Defining Literature

A Student's Guide

Defining Literature

A Student's Guide

Don Munro

Pearson Australia
(a division of Pearson Australia Group Pty Ltd)
707 Collins Street, Melbourne, Victoria 3008
PO Box 23360, Melbourne, Victoria 8012
www.pearson.com.au

First published 2000 by Pearson Australia
2018 2017 2016 2015
26 25 24 23 21

Designed by Lucy Adams
Set in Giovanni Book 8/10.5pt by Kimberly Taliai, Blue Orange
Edited by Jay Dale

Produced by Pearson Australia
Printed in Australia by the SOS Print + Media Group

National Library of Australia

Munro, Don.

Defining Literature: A Student's Guide.

Includes index.
ISBN 978-0-7339-0812-5

1. English literature - Terminology. I. Title.

820.9
Pearson Australia Group Pty Ltd ABN 40 004 245 943

The publishers would like to thank the following for permission to reproduce material in this book:

'The Dry Salvages' from *Four Quartets* by T.S. Eliot, p. 14

Cartoon © Mary Leunig, from *There's No Place Like Home*, 1982, p. 88

Cartoons © by Judy Horacek, reprinted with permission from *If the Fruit Fits*, Hodder Headline Australia, 1999, pp. 16, 46, 83, 95

Cartoons © by Judy Horacek, reprinted with permission from *Woman with Altitude*, Hodder Headline Australia, 1998, pp. 10, 43, 47, 49, 53, 77

The Scream by Edvard Munch. Photo: J. Lathion, © Nasjonalgalleriet, p. 40

The lines from 'The Knight' Copyright © 1993, 1967, 1963 by Adrienne Rich. The lines from 'Implosions' Copyright © 1993 by Adrienne Rich. Copyright © 1969 by W.W. Norton and Company, Inc, from *Collected Early Poems: 1950–1970* by Adrienne Rich. Used by permission of the author and W.W. Norton & Company, Inc.

Every effort has been made to trace and acknowledge copyright. However, should any infringement have occurred, the publishers tender their apologies and invite copyright owners to contact them.

Introduction

Defining Literature: A Student's Guide has been written for students in the upper-secondary school, although students at middle secondary level and university will find it a valuable resource in their study of literature, language and culture.

New terms and Student examples

This glossary of literature terms includes those terms that have only recently been introduced to English courses in Australia especially in the 'Viewing' strand of the Outcomes and Standards Framework. As with most glossaries, it is impossible to include every term featured; therefore, terms have been carefully selected from the syllabuses of several Australian states, with the text concentrating on simple definitions and examples of clear and accurate student usage. It is the student examples that will prove most useful to students, as most of the examples not only show how the term is used, but put it into a useful context as well.

Test your understanding

Some of the entries have an added short test of understanding; allowing students to check their understanding of the definition they have just read.

Index

The Index (listed by author's name and film's title) will be of use to students who want to find out what entries apply to the texts they are studying.

Acknowledgements

Many thanks to all the students who contributed work to this glossary. In particular, I'd like to thank:

Margaret Stevenson of John Curtin Senior High School for her stylish writing
Emma Gill
Carla Wright
Kate Johnson
Brooke Longville
Leah Crichton
Edward Gnanapragasm
Brooke Goddard
James McHale
Samantha O'Neill
Teneille Thorpe
Jessica Desmond
all of Willetton Secondary High School for their interest, inspiration and hard work.

A special thanks to my wife, Marie, for all her support and assistance.

Don Munro 2000

Aa

Aboriginal literature

Texts (often oral) created by the indigenous peoples of Australia.

These texts are usually about Aboriginal life and culture. Many of them are stories from the Dreamtime.

Aboriginal songs and chants are about particular places and spaces, and include such things as long-held cultural myths, maps to find significant sites, and directions on how to go about daily matters of life.

> **Student example**
> Aboriginal literature is a difficult term, since most of the texts are oral and they do not follow the usual conventions of poetry or narrative. Like most writers, Oodgeroo Noonuccal has had to adapt her poetry to be understood and have it considered as 'literature'.

absurdism

The literary movement that grew from the disillusion after the Second World War.

This was a rejection of the traditional values and beliefs that humankind was a rational creature who lived in a universe that was mostly comprehensible, and that social order, civilisation and dignity were possible. So, absurdist literature represents humankind as alone in a random and incomprehensible universe, leading a meaningless, even laughable, existence without hope or dignity. Some of the best known works are Samuel Beckett's *Waiting for Godot*, Jean-Paul Sartre's *Nausea* and Albert Camus' *The Outsider*.

Camus, in his *The Myth of Sisyphus*, draws a parallel between the fates of the Ancient Greek King Sisyphus and humankind. The Ancient Greek myth explains that the king, when confronted by Death, cheated him several times so that he was able to live to a ripe old age and die of natural causes. When he finally entered the Underworld, Hades set him a terrible punishment. He had to roll a large and heavy rock up a hill, trying to get it to sit on the very top of the hill. But every time he got the rock near the top of the hill it would roll back down again, and he would have to start all over again. Some commentators see this as symbolic of our attempts to gain knowledge.

See Theatre of the Absurd, existential philosophy.

acronym

An acronym is a word or abbreviation formed from the initial letters of a group of words; for example: EFTPOS is an acronym for 'electronic funds transfer at point of sale' and WACA is an acronym for West Australian Cricket Association.

> **Test your understanding**
> What are the acronyms for:
>
> 1 World Health Organisation?
> 2 Compact Disk-Read Only Memory?
> 3 Agnetha Bjorn Benny Anni-Frid?

act

A major section of a play.

In Elizabethan drama, plays were generally written in five acts. Ibsen and Chekhov wrote their plays in four acts. Many modern plays are written in three acts: the first act is seen as the exposition, the second is the complication, the third is the climax and resolution.

Scenes are smaller sections within acts and are usually divided from each other by a change of setting. Acts are divided from each other by a change in the development of the plot. Some modern dramas have abandoned act and scene divisions altogether, seeing them as unnecessary or artificial pauses. However, only short plays can avoid giving the audience an intermission break somewhere near the middle of the action!

See scene.

active voice/passive voice

Writing that uses the forms of verbs which create a direct and active relationship between the subject and the object. For example: 'We had fun' is written in the active voice; 'Fun was had' is written in the passive voice.

Usually it is best to use the active voice because it is livelier and more direct. But sometimes the passive is unavoidable—even preferable. If we write 'The whole class supported my idea' that is active and specific. But if we don't know how many students supported it (perhaps it was only the vocal ones) then we would be more justified in writing 'My idea was supported'.

Test your understanding
Write these active sentences into the passive voice.

1 The principal will prosecute trespassers.
2 Board members have reserved these seats.

aesthetics

The philosophy of our responses to works of art and literature.

Aesthetics considers such questions as: What is beauty? Is beauty and artistic merit only in the eye of the beholder? Can critical judgements of art and literature be objective?

affective fallacy

The error of judging a text by the effect it has on its readers.

This idea was proposed by the new critics Wimsatt and Beardsley in 1946. They have subsequently retracted the notion, since, Beardsley agrees, there can be no objective criticism.
See reading, objective/subjective.

affect/affective response

Texts affect readers, that is, they produce an intellectual and emotional response in their readers.

An affective response can be contrasted to a critical response, that is, the affective response focuses on describing the reader's reactions to the text without concern for the way in which they arose. The critical response will add to this an analysis of the way the text is working to position the reader through its use of various techniques.

Student example A
I was greatly affected by the final scenes of Titanic. The huge loss of life was itself a reason to grieve, but the noble and dignified way that most people faced their death made me feel a sense of pride in being human.

Student example B
I was deeply moved by the end of the film—the way the director focused on the tearing apart of family groups with close-ups of the women's and children's faces as they were lowered away from their husbands and fathers; this really increased the impact and pathos of those final scenes.

Age of Reason

The Restoration and Augustan periods. So called because it was a time in which reason and rational thinking was greatly revered.

Alexandrine

A line of poetry of twelve syllables.

This is a very popular meter in French poetry. In English poetry it seems too long as Pope pointed out in his 'Essay on Criticism':

a needless Alexandrine ends the song;
That, like a wounded snake, drags its slow length along.

allegory

An allegory can be seen as an extended metaphor—a text which invites interpretations on at least two levels.

Student example
This student response to George Orwell's well-known novel *Animal Farm* illustrates the idea.

One reading of this novel is at the level of subject matter. An entire farmyard of animals overthrow their human master and attempt to run the farm themselves, treating every animal as equal. The text also invites another reading at the historical level. I can read this story as an exploration of the events and ideas involved in the Russian Revolution of 1917 and the end of Orwell's novel might even be seen as a forecast of the downfall of Russian Communism...

So it can be said, an allegory invites the reader to make intertextual connections between large sections (or even the whole) of the text and some other text. These connections can be at different levels such as political, historical or cultural.

alliteration

The repetition of the consonant sounds at the beginnings of words.

It is often used to produce a sound that adds to the atmosphere or mood of the words, or perhaps even echoes their meaning. For example:

The fair breeze blew, the white foam flew,
The furrow followed free

from 'The Rime of the Ancient Mariner' by Samuel Taylor Coleridge; and 'Fish, flesh or fowl, commend all summer long...' from 'Sailing to Byzantium' by W. B. Yeats. Both use the 'f' sound to evoke a sense of activity and perhaps reinforce the sound of the wind. Adrienne Rich uses a whirl of 'w's' as an epigraph for her poem 'Implosions':

The world's
not wanton
only wild and wavering

allusion

A reference to another text, person, place or event.

This is usually used to clarify an idea or enhance meaning. The playful advertisement for a brand of bathers showed pictures of their new products with the voice-over warning us: 'Just when you thought it was safe to go back in the water...'. Most people in the TV audience understood the allusion to the promotional line for the film *Jaws 2* and laughed (or at least smiled).

Allusions can be the fairly obvious and direct kind such as Anthony Hecht's poem 'The Dover Bitch' which is clearly alluding to Matthew Arnold's poem 'Dover Beach'.

Sometimes allusions can be indirect and fairly difficult to pick up; for example: Lewis Carroll's narrative poem 'The Hunting of the Snark' is subtitled 'An Agony in Eight Fits'. The 'Agony' refers to the ancient usage of the word meaning 'a struggle that involves anguish and pain'. It could also be an allusion to Coleridge's poem 'The Rime of the Ancient Mariner' and the 'woeful agony' that grips the old sailor as he retells his tale. This would be a useful connection to make, since Carroll's poem is also about a long voyage that ends in death and angst.

See intertextuality.

Test your understanding

What is being alluded to in the following examples:

1 Prince was a great fighting dog but he met his Waterloo last week.
2 Mr Johnson won't sponsor you. He's a real Scrooge.
3 Robert Frost's poem 'Out, Out—' creates a sense of the absurdity and brevity of life.
4 'look!
up in the sky.
it's a bird.
it's a plane.
no...
it's Superwog.'
(extract from 'Superwog' by Komninos)

alternative reading

A reading of a text that takes a different approach to the dominant reading, but does not challenge the assumptions of that reading.

Student example A

'The Three Little Pigs' is a story that warns us to make sensible provisions for the future. The first two pigs are victims of their own laziness and lack of forethought. Only the third little pig has put in the thought and the work that protects it against the wolf.

Student example B

'The Three Little Pigs' shows us that some cultures are superior to others due to their technological advancement. Only brick buildings are permanent enough to withstand the wild and savage forces of nature. Cultures that haven't made that progress will not survive.

Test your understanding

Which of these is the dominant reading? Which do you think is the alternative reading? Explain your reasoning.

ambiguity

A word or phrase that invites at least two interpretations.

In act 2, scene 2 of Shakespeare's *Hamlet*, the prince deliberately misinterprets Polonius's words (not taking 'matter' to mean 'printed matter' but 'problem'):

Polonius: What do you read my lord?
Hamlet: Words, words, words!
Polonius: What is the matter, my lord?
Hamlet: Between who?
Polonius: I mean the matter that you read, my lord.

In act 3, scene 2, Hamlet uses ambiguity at poor Ophelia's expense. He seems to deliberately invite Ophelia to interpret 'lie in your lap' with a sexual overtone:

Hamlet: Lady, shall I lie in your lap?
Ophelia: No, my lord.
Hamlet: I mean my head upon your lap?
Ophelia: Ay, my lord.
Hamlet: Do you think I meant country matters?
Ophelia: I think nothing my lord.

anachronism

Something which is out of its time.

One of the classic examples is Shakespeare's mention of billiards in *Antony and Cleopatra*. The play is set around 30 BC. Billiards (as we know the game) was first described in the seventeenth century AD. A popular example of anachronism is in the comic 'Asterix the Gaul'. Here it is used for humorous effect, as the scene when Asterix has a cup of tea with the ancient Briton Boadicea is set around 50 BC, and tea was not brought to Europe until the late sixteenth century AD.

In Shakespeare's *Julius Caesar* (act 2, scene 1, lines 193–4) Brutus is a nervous conspirator and asks his friend Cassius for the time:

Brutus: Peace! Count the clock.
Cassius: The clock has stricken three.

The first mechanical clocks were seen in Rome about 1400 years later, although some defenders of Shakespeare might argue that Brutus was referring to a water clock, which was in use at the time.

anagram

A word or phrase whose letters have been rearranged to form a new word or phrase.

Two famous anagrams are Samuel Butler's novel title *Erehwon* (the name of an imagined land) and Dylan Thomas's name for the town in *Under Milkwood*—'Llareggub'. Both of these only need to be read backwards. Another anagram is 'Flit on cheering angel' for Florence Nightingale.

anagnorisis

The moment in a tragedy when the tragic hero realises what they have done and what the irreversible consequences will be.

This occurs in *Macbeth* when he realises that all the witches' prophecies have come true and that they have tricked him by their 'double talk'. In *Oedipus Rex*, this is when Oedipus realises that it is he who killed his own father and that he must bear the punishment that he, as king, decreed.

See tragic hero.

analogy

A comparison made between two things that share something in common.

Earth might be compared to a soccer ball to illustrate the idea of rotation about an axis. Analogy is often used in poetry to help us see something familiar in a new light. Seamus Heaney, in his poem 'Digging', compares his pen to a spade and makes us think again about the way his poetry works by concluding: 'I'll dig with it'.

analysis

Literally, this means taking something apart to see how it works.

The opposite of analysis is synthesis, combining elements to see what it looks like as a whole. The analysis of text involves looking at the way it has been constructed in terms of its use of techniques or conventions, and examining the way those techniques influence the overall interpretation and response. A good analysis does not mean 'killing' the text by leaving it lying around in bits and pieces, but it should bring the text more into the light so that we can see exactly how it is operating and understand more clearly the version of the world it is presenting to us.

One method of analysing a poem might go like this:

- examine a meaning and your initial response
- expose the techniques used (persona, sound devices, structure, imagery, etc.)
- show how these techniques influence your response (how they position you as a reader)
- state the values that the poem presents
- outline your acceptance or rejection of that position and your final response to the poem.

If you use a model like this one, you will avoid one of the major problems students encounter in writing analyses of texts—merely identifying the techniques the text uses without being able to show what effect such techniques have on the reader's response. The first student has fallen into that trap.

Student example A

In the poem 'Nightfall in Soweto' Oswald Mbuyiseni Mtshali personifies the night to be something frightening that is hunting him down. He uses a lot of metaphors and similes to back this up: his house is a matchbox, the hunter is like a rabid dog, and it has become a marauding beast to run him down. The poem does not rhyme, but keeps up a rapid rhythm and pace because of its short lines and short stanzas.

All these are valid observations to make in an analysis, but they are not telling us anything about the way the reader is responding to the text—it is merely observing techniques and labelling them. This second student does better.

Student example B

Mtshali personifies the night. It becomes 'cruel', hunting the persona down—even to his home which is described as a 'matchbox house', something small and easily crushed. The power and determination of nightfall, and the powerlessness of its victims makes this a frightening and compelling poem about the violence experienced by Blacks in South Africa.

See critical analysis.

anecdote/anecdotal evidence

An anecdote is a small story that illustrates a point.

Anecdotes are often used to introduce essays or newspaper feature articles. Sue Chessborough begins her feature article about grandparents who have lost their grandchildren like this:

> It all began when my daughter, Kris, went to visit a remote Greek island for three days...

Anecdotal evidence is usually thought of as a poor substitute for 'real evidence'—it relies on an individual case to make a point, and as the listeners or readers may respond: 'It's the exception that proves the rule'. An argument in favour of smoking that relies on anecdotal evidence like 'My grandfather smoked for 47 years and he never developed cancer' is pretty easy to dismiss.

See argument.

annotation

A comment on the text.

This might be made by a reader in the margins of a book. The term 'marginalia' also describes these notes. An editor who wishes to explain the meaning of a text or provide background information may write annotations and publish them as an addition to the original text. Martin Gardner's editions of *Alice in Wonderland* and *The Hunting of the Snark* are excellent examples of texts with very entertaining annotations. Students might also be familiar with some Shakespearean texts with annotations on facing pages.

antagonist

The character or agent in a narrative play or film who opposes the main character or protagonist.

The words antagonist and protagonist are derived from Greek: *agon* means contest, *pro* means for, or in favour of, and *anti* means against. So the contest between these two elements is the conflict between good and evil. Darth Vader is the antagonist to Luke Skywalker (the protagonist) in *Star Wars*. Farfrae is the antagonist to Henchard in *The Mayor of Casterbridge*.

One way of looking at the functions of these two characters is to regard the protagonist as someone who wants to solve a problem and the antagonist is the force that opposes those efforts.

See conflict.

Test your understanding
Who is the protagonist, who is the antagonist, and what is each trying to achieve in the following stories?

1 'The Three Little Pigs'
2 'Little Red Riding Hood'
3 'Jesus in the Wilderness'

anthology

A collection of texts.

This term comes from the Greek meaning 'a collection of flowers', which perhaps explains the effect most editors would hope to achieve with their anthologies. Originally, in Ancient Greece, anthologies were collections of epigrams (wise sayings). Nowadays, they can be collections of poems, stories, jokes, almost anything.

anticlimax

A point in a narrative that promises to be the climax and then fails to deliver.

In anticlimax, as opposed to climax, issues and problems are not resolved, the truth is not revealed, and perhaps certain characters who we thought were going to change, do not.

Anticlimax can be used to delay the real climax, but it must be used carefully or it will result in a comic deflation. The popular usage of the term conveys this feeling of disappointment.

Student example
When Chrissy is about to go on national TV to tell the world about the STARK conspiracy she is introduced as a 'daft dingo'—an anticlimax since we know she will convince no-one with that introduction.

anti-hero

A protagonist or main character who does not provoke admiration or sympathy in the reader because their dominant qualities are not attractive.

Thomas Covenant (in Stephen Donaldson's *The Chronicles of Thomas Covenant, The Unbeliever*) is an anti-hero because he does not believe that the world in which he finds himself is real, and is consequently alienated from, and indifferent to, the world and people around him.

Other well-known examples of characters who do not display the qualities we would expect from a 'hero' are Yossarian in Joseph Heller's *Catch 22*, Jimmy Porter in John Osborne's play *Look Back in Anger* and Charles in the film *Four Weddings and a Funeral*.

See hero/heroine.

Test your understanding
Contrast the qualities of an anti-hero you have encountered with these well-known heroes:

1 Luke Skywalker: idealistic, self-sacrificing, quick to learn, fighting for freedom
2 Indiana Jones: intelligent, brave, ingenious, fighting for good and democracy
3 Romeo: impulsive, brave, passionate, fighting for love and justice

antithesis

Setting up an opposition of contrasting ideas in a phrase or sentence. For example: 'Help yourself, and Heaven will help you' (Jean de la Fontaine); and 'Marriage has many pains, but celibacy has no pleasures' (Dr Johnson).

antonym

Antonyms are words with opposite meanings; for example: black/white, positive/negative, brave/cowardly.

See binary opposition.

aphorism

A short and pithy statement, for example: 'knowledge is power'.

apocalypse

A vision of the end of the world, often involving war and great natural disasters.

The Four Horsemen of the Apocalypse are four horrible humanoid figures on horseback representing war, famine, pestilence and death.

apostrophe

This word has two meanings: a punctuation mark (usually used to show ownership or to indicate a contraction); or a figure of speech.

As a figure of speech, it is used to address

someone dead or absent, or some thing, as if they were capable of understanding. A well-known example is Wordsworth's appeal to the dead poet in his poem 'London 1812': 'Milton! Thou shouldst be living at this hour…'.

See invocation.

Arcadia

Originally a mountainous region of Greece used by poets as the symbol for the ideal pastoral life.

In its early white settlement, Australia was thought to be an Arcadia.

archetypes

Characters or ideas that share a recognisable pattern.

Some well-known archetypes are the hero fighting for a good cause, against all odds; the innocent, uninitiated boy; and the important object that must be rescued from evil.

See stereotype.

Student example

Iago is the archetypal villain. He is manipulative, deceitful and lacks a conscience.

Test your understanding

Identify the characters from *Star Wars, Episode 1* that best fit the archetypes described above.

argument

There are two useful definitions: a summary of the plot or content of a chapter in a book; and the series of reasoned steps that lead from several premises to a conclusion.

The first definition was a popular technique used in seventeenth and eighteenth century writing.

Referring to the second definition, an argument in an essay must be logical, clearly explained or reasoned, supported by evidence (either facts and figures or quotes and references to texts), and aptly sequenced (the points should be in a suitable order).

See evidence, conclusion.

article

A short piece of prose, often found in newspapers or magazines.

Most articles are based on fact or actual events, but they will present a particular view of their subject, depending on the writer's perspective.

See feature article.

aside

Words or lines spoken for the benefit of the audience or a particular character but which other characters on stage cannot hear.

These lines reveal the character's thoughts, feelings or motivations. This is an excellent example of a convention since, clearly, all the characters on stage would be able to hear the aside. As an audience we understand the rules of this technique and accept the idea. In act 1, scene 3 of *Macbeth* by William Shakespeare, Macbeth is stunned by the predictions of the witches and separates his reactions for different audiences. The first aside is only for himself and the audience to hear:

Macbeth:	(Aside) Glamis and Thane of Cawdor: The greatest is behind.
(To Ross and Angus):	Thanks for your pains.
(Aside to Banquo):	Do you not hope your children shall be kings…

Student example

One of the most effective methods used to reveal the thoughts and feelings of Macbeth is in the aside. We are able to hear his alarmed reaction to the witches' prophecies when he says: 'This supernatural soliciting cannot be ill, cannot be good…'. Whereas the other characters can only see his behaviour; Banquo makes this clear when he says: 'Look how our partner's rap't' (line 142) which means that the other characters on stage have noticed Macbeth thinking (or talking to himself?) and wonder what he is doing.

assonance

The repetition of a vowel sound to create a particular effect.

One of these effects may be to produce a pleasant sound pattern as in, 'Those who have seen thee seeking know thee well'. The 'ee' sound in 'seen', 'thee' and 'seek' are in assonance and create a pleasant effect on the ear.

Another effect of assonance can be to lengthen the sound of a line or to slow down its pace. Seamus Heaney uses this technique in his poem 'Death of a Naturalist':

Right down the dam gross-bellied frogs were cocked
On sods; their loose necks pulsed like sails. Some hopped:
The slap and plop were obscene threats...

The student (Rita) in *Educating Rita* has a more humorous view of such repeated sounds. Here she discusses 'assonance' with her tutor (Frank):

Frank: ...there's a Yeats poem, called 'The Wild Swans at Coole'. In it he rhymes the word 'swan' with the word 'stone'. There, you see, an example of assonance.
Rita: Oh. It means gettin' the rhyme wrong.

This is even more humorous since the teacher has quoted an example of consonance, getting it wrong himself.

See consonance.

assumptions

Things that are taken for granted, suppositions that are used as an often unstated basis for an argument or a reading position.

Texts make assumptions about many things; for example: who is reading it, the subject and people under discussion, and the codes and conventions of the culture it presents.

Test your understanding
Read the text from *Coping with Computing* on page 86. Write down some of the assumptions the writers have made about the reader. If you need help to do this, *see* reading.

atmosphere

The mood created by the language of a text.

In film, the images and soundtrack can be used to create a particular atmosphere. The opening scenes of *Edward Scissorhands* show an over-run, neglected garden and a dilapidated castle with its walls and roof in a state of collapse. The music reinforces our growing anxiety, and the extended pan and dolly shots keep our view restricted; the atmosphere is tense and eerie. The same effect can be achieved in print texts.

Student example
Sonya Hartnett creates an eerie atmosphere of wilful neglect, something like the feeling of Haversham house in Dickens's *Great Expectations*, when she describes what has happened to the house on the Willow's farm:

When the house was grand...
(Now) The walls are scribbled upon...the (lino) is rucked and split like wounds.

The words 'rusted', 'rucked' and 'split' create a feeling of neglect and decay. Underneath this, words like 'scarred' and 'wounds' suggest a sense of threat and possible violence.

attitude

Literally, this means orientation, the manner in which something is positioned (a physical or mental position).

A spaceship has an attitude to an approaching planet. This is helpful when you need to distinguish attitudes from values. Values (the ideals or standards upon which actions are based) will usually determine your attitude to a subject. For example: one of your key values might be 'the fundamental importance of life above all other considerations' which produces predictable attitudes towards abortion and war. In Hans Peter Richter's novel *I Was There*, set in Germany in the days leading up to the Second World War, Heinz expresses his attitude towards the work of the Brown Shirts, the S.A. Sturm: 'The Brown Shirts, they know how to get things done!' This attitude arises from his belief that the Brown Shirts are working for the good of all Germans. Perhaps he values the security of the State above the rights and safety of individuals in it.

Because of this relationship between values, beliefs and attitudes it is important for readers to interrogate texts and explore their attitudes to the subject matter. Only then can readers challenge and accept or reject the value-position they are being asked to participate in while they are reading the text.

In the following examples of student writing one student has done this. The other has allowed the text to 'operate' on him without challenge.

Student example A

The poem 'Spring and Fall' by Gerard Manley Hopkins is a lesson for the young girl, Margaret, who is crying over the trees losing their leaves... The poem ends by explaining to Margaret the real reason for her tears: 'It is Margaret you mourn for'.

Student example B

This poem is an address from an adult to a child, Margaret. The adult assumes that he understands the reasons for the child's tears and condescends to explain this to her. Whether he is right or not we cannot judge (the poem invites us to assume he is) but I think it is misuse of power to blight a childhood with stories of her own death.

audience

Those to whom a text is addressed.

However, this idea is not as simple as it sounds. A poem like 'My Last Duchess' by Robert Browning has at least two kinds of audience: the messenger to whom the Duke is speaking and the readers who read the written text. To distinguish these different audiences the first might be called the addressee—the person or persons being directly addressed by the addresser, the person assumed to be speaking. The audience reading the text can be considered in more detail too. To understand more about this kind of audience read the text from *Coping with Computing* on page 86.

Now the reading audience of this text can be anyone who chooses to read it. But, who is the imagined audience? For example: is the text addressed to young women? Or, to left handers? Clearly the text has a preferred reading audience of right-handed married men.

The following student example shows how this idea can be used productively.

Student example

Robert Browning's poem 'My Last Duchess' is a dramatic monologue delivered by the Duke of Ferrara. It appears that he is addressing a messenger from the Count on the matter of marriage to his daughter. We, as the reading audience, are allowed to eavesdrop on his monologue, which becomes more and more frightening as it progresses.

audience expectations

Things that the readers of a text anticipate that they will encounter in that text, usually generated from past experiences with similar texts.

A reader generates expectations of a text from all sorts of sources: the cover and blurb of a book, previews of TV shows and films, advertising about the text, other readers' responses, and previous experiences with texts of the same type.

A good reader usually holds many expectations when reading a text. Part of the enjoyment of reading is in forming expectations and finding out if they are fulfilled or not, later on in the text. The most obvious example of this occurs when we read a detective novel, a 'whodunit'. We are constantly evaluating the suspects and forming notions about who did it and why, until finally it is revealed at the end; and our guesses, hypotheses and expectations are rewarded or disappointed.

Another set of expectations arise from our previous experiences of reading texts of the same genre or type; for example: when we are reading an article in *Time* magazine or the *Australian* newspaper we expect the facts and figures to be reasonably accurate, although that expectation does not transfer to other newspapers such as a tabloid newspaper like the *Sun*, especially when their headline announces that a statue of Elvis has been found on Mars! The kind of expectations that we hold about different newspapers means that we will read them differently.

See intertextuality.

Augustan age

The period in English history around the end of the seventeenth century to the middle of the eighteenth century when the writers (such as Dryden, Swift, Pope and Johnson) imitated the style of the Roman poets who flourished in the reign of the Emperor Augustus (27 BC–AD 14).

Australian culture
The order, law, communication, art and social practices of the Australian community.

This definition already highlights some of the problems in using a concept like this. For example: which laws—Aboriginal tribal laws? Or, the laws of state or federal governments? Whose art—American TV soaps? An ABC TV documentary? The Country and Western Hour on ABC radio? Or, the music on Triple J? There are so many different groups with different customs and backgrounds in Australia that it must be impossible to describe them all in one simple definition of Australian culture.

The important things to remember, if you use this term, are that Australian culture is made up of many different peoples and groups and not all members of that culture share the same values, and that the Australian culture is continually changing.

It is, however, still possible to make some broad generalisations about the dominant culture in Australia in the twentieth century: the majority of its peoples are white of European origins, they share Christian values and beliefs, their laws are based on British law, and their art has grown from European roots. Just keep in mind that such descriptions can actually obscure more than they reveal. The student example illustrates one of the problems you might encounter when using this term.

Student example

In his poem 'The Not-so-good Earth' Bruce Dawe criticises one of the typical aspects of Australian culture. He describes the family as apathetic about the problems of the rest of the world...

Of course, Dawe might reply to this student that he wasn't making this criticism of all Australians—especially those that have come from other parts of the world, maintain close links with their homelands and take great interest in what is going on there.

See culture.

author
The creator of a text or object.

The process by which authors create texts is worth considering. Authors construct texts. They make choices about what things or ideas to put into their texts, and what things or ideas they will leave out. They also select the words and phrases they will use to express these ideas. In all these cases, they are selecting from a paradigm, that is, from the group of all the possible choices available to them. The choices they make will depend on the kind of effect they are hoping to have on their audience. A simple example can be seen in the film *Titanic*. The American director/ writers had a large number of facts to choose from when they made the film. One of the more interesting facts that they left out was that an American ship, *Californian*, was drifting less than 12 miles away from the sinking *Titanic*. This ship did not respond to the distress calls and flares. These facts were included in an earlier film version (*A Night to Remember*) of the sinking of the *Titanic*. Why might this have been left out of the 1997 version? Perhaps the authors didn't want the audience to see Americans portrayed in such a tragic and embarrassing situation? Whatever their reasons, their choice to omit this material has affected the way we respond to the sinking of the ship and the huge loss of life.

Student example

In Ken Kirby's documentary *Savagery and the American Indian*, our first impression from the title may be that this will be a documentary about some of the savage practices of the American Indians, like scalping. However, after we've seen the film, we realise that the savagery he was referring to was that of the invading Europeans. This explains his choice of the word 'and' in the title, rather than 'of' and reminds us, very simply, of the position from which he wants us to view these issues.

See intentional fallacy.

authority

The credibility that an author creates or claims through the statements that are made in a text.

Most texts try to create the sense that their writers know what they are writing about, whether they do or not. Readers will judge whether the text creates and maintains this sense of authority or not.

author's context

The situation or surrounding circumstances in which the author creates the text.

These circumstances can be seen as:

- historical (the time when it was written)
- geographical (the place and/or country where it was written)
- cultural (the author's background, for example: is she an English working class writer who has often written about women's rights and issues?)
- religious (does the religion of the writer have any effect on the text?).

There are other factors to consider depending on the author who is in focus, for example: social context, economic circumstances, age, gender, etc. The author's context is often worth exploring when we read a text. Although we would not do this to figure out what the author meant when they wrote the text (*see* intentional fallacy), we can come to a better understanding of how some factors in the author's circumstances have contributed to the way the text was created. For example: this student has been able to see a connection between John Donne's poem 'Elegie: To his Mistris Going To Bed', and the historical context of the writer.

Student example

The speaker of the poem is an Englishman of the seventeenth century. His excitement mounts when he compares his mistress to America: 'my America, my new found land'. This is a reflection of the tenor of the times. Such discoveries as America and the other new British colonies brought exotic new products into British homes and a consequent pride in Britain's power. Donne feels a similar power in his relationship with his mistress.

See new historicism.

autobiography

An account of a person's life, written from their perspective.

This contrasts with a biography which is written by someone other than the subject of the text. Autobiographies are narrative because they tell the story of the person's life (or part of it).

avant-garde

Those in the front.

In art and literature this is applied to those making bold experiments or pushing at the known boundaries of their art.

axiom

A basic principle—often taken as given, not requiring proof.

Student example

That a documentary presents us with a particular version of reality is axiomatic.

Bb

ballad

A song or poem that tells a story—traditionally transmitted orally.

A good example of the earliest types of ballads is 'Sir Patrick Spens'. The last stanza illustrates some of the main features of the ballad form:

Half-owre, half-owre to Aberdour,
'Tis fifty fathoms deep;
And there lies gude Sir Patrick Spens,
Wi' the Scots lords at his feet!

This ballad tries to preserve some of its original flavour by keeping the Scottish accent in the language. Many of the early ballads capture local accents and colour. There is also a strong rhyme and rhythm in this stanza. There's a strong internal rhyme in the first line ('owre' and 'Aberdour') and the second and fourth lines rhyme (in this case it is assonance). The four-line stanza (quatrain) uses short lines with a regular rhythm. The repetition in the first line ('half-owre', meaning half-hour) is also a common technique used by ballads to produce dramatic emphasis, and to make the whole poem a little easier to remember and recite.

bard

A poet of note.

In ancient Celtic tradition, bards were appointed by kings or princes to write and recite poetry to celebrate notable events. In Wales this tradition still lives on in the Eisteddfod (a cultural fair). Sometimes Shakespeare is referred to as 'the bard'.

bathos

An attempt at passionate or lofty writing that overshoots the mark and produces, instead, a comic or trivial effect.

For example: 'I am ready to sacrifice myself', she declared, 'for God, my country and my suburb!' The anonymous poet who wrote 'A Rondeau on Black Eyes' provides another example:

By two black eyes my heart was won,
Sure never wretch was more undone.
To Celia with my suit I came,
But she, regardless of her prize,
Thought proper to reward my flame
With two black eyes!

Beat generation poetry

The poetry that originated from San Francisco in the 1950s and 1960s.

It is often described as the poetry of the American Renaissance—a rebirth of art, music and literature centred in the San Francisco night life. Ginzberg, Corso and Ferlinghetti are three of the more widely known poets to emerge from this era. Most of their poetry is in free verse, using very earthy language and imagery, often dealing with issues that the previous generations would not approve of—drugs, sex and the problems of living in big cities. Allen Ginzberg's 'Howl' is memorable. It begins:

I saw the best minds of my generation
destroyed by madness, starving hysterical,
naked...

belief

A conscious decision to support an idea, despite the fact that it cannot be proved beyond all doubt.

Some cynical observers of life have described it as 'the stubborn refusal to abandon an idea despite all evidence to the contrary'. Beliefs can range from something on which you base your life, for example: the belief that working harder will bring better results, or the belief that eating meat is wrong; to the trivial, the belief that Friday the 13th is unlucky.

A set of beliefs that explain the way the world works or describe the way of thinking of a particular group of people is called an 'ideology'. Some of the important beliefs of our Australian culture are the belief in a Christian God, the value of education, the fundamental importance of the family, and the unequal distribution of wealth and power.

See attitude.

bias

A leaning to one side because more weight is placed on that side.

A lawn bowl has a bias so that it rolls in a curve, rather than a straight line. To accuse a person of bias (to say they are biased) is to say they have not got the facts of the case in proper balance, and that they favour one side of an argument unfairly. To suggest that a writer is biased on an issue implies that their opinion is not supported by the facts.

All this is, of course, problematic for it suggests that the person who is accusing the writer of bias has access to all the facts—that they can see the issue objectively. The best we can say is that readers and writers hold particular values and beliefs, and they may not always coincide. To describe writers who express opinions opposed to ours as biased is to misuse the word—it should be reserved for those who can be shown to deliberately distort the evidence.

> **Student example**
> E. P. France in his letter to the editor shows real bias against the Aborigines. He claims that '... they are all descendants of the slaves and slave traders who were shipwrecked along the Australian coast in earlier centuries and they worship pagan gods'. This is not supported by the facts of Aboriginal descent. Nor are all Aborigines pagans—many are Christians.

bibliography

A list of resources (books, newspapers, films, etc.) used as references for a particular subject.

Bibliographies are organised according to a strict set of rules so that readers can easily interpret them. They are usually placed at the end of an essay or article.

See quotation.

Bildungsroman

A novel that describes the youthful development of a character or characters.

This term comes from the German and literally means 'formation novel'. Some famous examples include James Joyce's *A Portrait of the Artist as a Young Man* and *Tom Jones* by Henry Fielding.

binary opposition

A pair of words or ideas that are polar opposites.

One of these ideas is usually preferred to the other; for example: good/bad, culture/nature, day/night, tame/feral.

See structuralism. *See* proposition (for a student example).

biography

A written account of a person's life.

This means that the writer attempts to tell the story of another person's life, usually in chronological order from birth to death. There is often an attempt to create character, motivations and temperament, and a sense of the times and places in which that person lived. Some biographies include *Life of Samuel Johnson* by James Boswell (1791), *Robert J. Hawke—A Biography* by Blanche d'Alpuget (1982) and *Careless Love: The Unmaking of Elvis Presley* by Peter Guralnick (1999).

black comedy

A form of humour recognisable by its cynicism and sense of bitter disillusionment with life.

Black Comedy is a product of the twentieth century and the literary and philosophical movements that saw life as a kind of sick joke, being short, meaningless and often painful. Black humour is most often found in Theatre of the Absurd, but it is also present in some of the literature of the surrealists and the existentialists like Jean Paul Sartre's novel *Nausea* or Joseph Heller's novel *Catch 22*.

See Theatre of the Absurd.

blank verse

Lines of unrhymed poetry in a regular rhythm (usually iambic pentameter).

This kind of poetry is called blank because there is no rhyme pattern. Its rhythms come closest to the rhythms of natural English speech, and it has been used by poets to imitate the way we think and speak. Shakespeare's plays are written mainly in blank verse; so is Wordsworth's 'Prelude', and T. S. Eliot's 'The Waste Land' and 'Four Quartets'.

This example is from T. S. Eliot's 'The Dry Salvages', part three of the 'Four Quartets'.

> Lady, whose shrine stands on the promontory,
> Pray for all those who are in ships, those
> Whose business has to do with fish, and
> Those concerned with every lawful traffic
> And those who conduct them.

This example is from Adrienne Rich's poem 'The Knight'.

> A knight rides into the noon
> and his helmet points to the sun
> and a thousand splintered suns
> are the gaiety of his mail...

blurb

The more or less truthful description of a book's contents on the back cover or flap.

The word is attributed to Belett Burgess, an American writer and editor who is reputed to have said, 'A blurb is a cheque drawn on fame, and is seldom honoured'.

books

Texts printed on paper and bound together.

They may be composed of words or illustrations, or both. This word is a problem for some students, as they use it to describe almost anything they read. It is not a good substitute for 'novel' or 'play', or any other specific genre, for although these texts may well be found in book form that is not what defines them. It is much better to describe these texts by their genre or category, because that begins to say something about the nature of the text.

> **Student example**
> *The Perfectionist* by David Williamson is a book about modern relationships.

It would be much better if this student was to refer to this text as a play script since the above statement prompts us to think of it as a 'do-it-yourself' handbook on love and marriage.

bowdlerise

To take out of a text everything that might offend delicate tastes.

Dr Bowdler produced a 'cleaned-up' version of Shakespeare's works. Needless to say, works like *Romeo and Juliet* became very brief indeed!

burlesque

A type of comedy in which the subjects or characters are made to appear ridiculous by the techniques of exaggeration and parody.

An early example includes the clowning antics of Bottom and his friends in Shakespeare's *A Midsummer Night's Dream*.

See comedy.

Cc

cadence

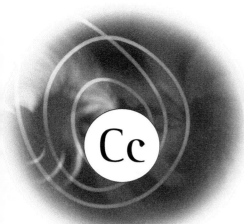

The natural sound of language.

The 'inner music' that you can hear when words are spoken or read. The cadence arises from the pattern of stressed and unstressed sounds, and the rising and falling tones inherent in the structure of sentences. All writing and speaking has this quality, and it varies from writer to writer. Some writers have such an easily identifiable cadence that readers can pick them by just reading a short paragraph and hearing their 'voice' in the sentences.

> **Student example**
> Matthew Arnold, in 'Dover Beach', creates a cadence that reflects the sombre nature of his thoughts:
>
> Listen! you hear the grating roar
> Of pebbles which the waves draw back, and
> fling,
> At their return, up the high strand,
> Begin, and cease, and then again begin...

See rhythm.

caesura

A definite pause in a line of verse, usually caused by pause marks such as the comma, the semi-colon or the colon, but the caesura can even be caused by a full stop in the middle of a line.

Its effect is to provide a change to the rhythm of the surrounding lines and give an emphasis on the words surrounding the caesura.

> **Student example**
> In Gerard Manley Hopkins' poem 'The Binsey Poplars' the third line contains two caesuras and that stops the flow of the previous line like two blows from an axe.
>
> My aspens dear, whose airy cages quelled,
> Quelled or quenched in leaves the leaping sun,
> All felled, felled, are all felled

> **Test your understanding**
> What are the effects of the caesuras in these lines from Robert Browning's poem 'Andrea del Sarto'?
>
> This chamber for example—turn your head—
> All that's behind us! You don't understand
> Nor care to understand about my art

camera position

The physical location of the camera at the time of shooting, including the focus, framing and angle of the shot.

In the making of a documentary or a feature film, the choice of camera positions will occupy the director's mind for some time, as they will influence the way the audience responds to the subject.

See carpe diem.

Student example

A student's answer to the question: 'How does the camera position influence the way we respond to the subject matter of Ken Kirby's *Savagery and the American Indian?*'

> In the opening scene of *Savagery and the American Indian*, the camera is positioned at eye-level and at a medium distance to the lone Indian. It dollies gently along beside him as he stalks some prey with a bow and arrow, creating interest in his intention and his target. A cut repositions the camera close to the edge of some undergrowth. Crashing out of that greenery is a large bearded white man with a gun, filmed at a low angle to make his sudden appearance even more startling. The use of the camera angle and distance has positioned us to regard the white man as a violent intruder in a natural and traditional scene.

canon

A body of texts that are thought to be of great literary worth.

Some of the writers that have appeared on most people's canons are Shakespeare, Dante, Austen, Tolstoy, Proust, Ibsen and Beckett. The difficulty with this idea is who is going to decide what texts should be on this list and what standards are they going to use when choosing? As Dale Spender observed, most canons are composed of texts written by white Anglo-Saxon males. Most modern critics question the validity of evaluating works of literature and ranking them; although, in practice, teachers and students are often selecting suitable texts for reading and study from a fairly narrow list called a syllabus text list!

See classic.

caricature

In literature, this term means the depiction of a character which exaggerates one or two of their qualities for the purposes of making fun of them.

carpe diem

Translated from the Latin this phrase means, 'seize the day'.

The term has been used to describe the kind of poetry that encourages readers to live life while they can—because life and beauty are so short! Robert Herrick's poem 'To the Virgins, To Make Much of Time' begins with the lines that sum up this idea:

> Gather ye rosebuds while ye may,
> Old time is still a-flying;

Andrew Marvell's poem 'To His Coy Mistress' exhorts his young lover to part with her virginity as quickly as possible: 'Now let us sport us while we may...'.

catastrophe

The tragic outcome of events in a tragedy.

The death of Prince Hamlet and the reappearance of the blind Oedipus are examples.

categories

Groups of things with some common characteristics.

Texts are often placed into categories by genre. The only difficulty in doing this is that once a text is placed in one category we have a tendency to only think of it in that way.

Texts can also be classified according to whether they are fiction or non-fiction, print or non-print, and many other opposing categories. The most interesting thing about such categories is that their boundaries are always being challenged by texts and readers. They are often found to be not as firm and fixed as we might first have thought. We find texts keep sliding between categories and some can belong in two or more categories at the same time. For example: the documentary film *Cane Toads* might be seen as a nature documentary about the introduction of the cane toad into Australia, but it could also be seen as a satire on Australian people and their attitudes to their environment. Is *Philadelphia* just a feature film about one man's struggle for justice? Or, do the documentary elements make it more a film about overcoming prejudice against people with AIDS? Is the feature film *Braveheart* a factual account of Scotland in the sixteenth century? Or, is it just a romanticised legend of William Wallace? Or, perhaps, it is a combination of the two?

This illustrates an important point about placing texts in categories—giving a text a label may have some value, but it is much more useful to explain what features you find in a text, and why you think that might place it in a particular genre or category.

Test your understanding
What categories or genres would you place these texts in?

1 *Star Wars Episode 1* (G. Lucas)
2 *Romeo and Juliet* (W. Shakespeare)
3 'Waltzing Matilda'
4 *Alice in Wonderland* (L. Carroll)

See genre.

catharsis

The release of emotions experienced by an audience towards the end of a tragedy.

Literally, this means a cleansing or purifying. The Ancient Greek philosopher, Aristotle, described this process as something that happens to an audience 'through pity and fear working a purification of these emotions'.

Student example
In Shakespeare's *Macbeth* we are gripped by fear at the witness of his downfall, because if such a great man as the Thane of Glamis can be overcome by the forces of darkness, then so can we. We are also full of pity for him when he has to meet his end—because, although he is in the grip of evil, and he has done some terrible things, he has showed himself to be a noble and brave man. At the moment he realises his fate and challenges it (and MacDuff) we experience a catharsis. Macbeth has regained his heroic nature and refuses to die a coward's death, and we are released from our pent-up pity and fear. We are cleansed.

See tragedy.

censorship

Banning parts or the whole of a text because it offends some element of morality or taste.

A text that has had some parts censored is called an 'expurgated text'. Walt Whitman said in 1888: 'Damn all expurgated books, the dirtiest book of all is the expurgated book'. The issue of censorship is a controversial one because it involves making judgements about texts, and different readers with different values will find themselves in conflict.
See bowdlerise.

characterisation

The methods used to create characters in a text.

There are five methods commonly used:

- direct description—when characters are created by description of their faces, clothing, personality, etc. Signora Mantucci is first described as:

> a small, fierce Sicilian woman with thick tinted glasses that enlarge her green eyes. She talks faster than any human I have ever heard...
>
> (Frances Mayes, *Under the Tuscan Sun* (1997))

- by their actions or speech—Ulysses is characterised by his firm decision in the poem by Tennyson:

> We are not now that strength which in old days
> Moved earth and heaven; that which we are, we are;
> One equal temper of heroic hearts,
> Made weak by time and fate, but strong in will
> To strive, to seek, to find, and not to yield.

- through their thoughts or feelings—nurse O'Halloran is characterised by her attitudes in *Angela's Ashes* by Frank McCourt:

> There is nurse O'Halloran, the midwife, all dressed up in her finery. It's New Year's Eve and Mrs O'Halloran is anxious for the child to be born so that she can rush off to the parties and celebrations...

- by what other characters say about them—Romeo is described by his father:

> But he, his own affections' counsellor,
> Is to himself — I will not say how true —
> But to himself so secret and so close...

  Which may be one of the causes of the tragedy of the young lovers.

- by symbolic association with particular objects or ideas—Theodora in Patrick White's *The Aunt's Story* is often associated with wood and bone, natural objects that are presented as symbolic of her good heart.

Student example

Even though we do not meet Kurtz until the end of Marlow's journey (in *Heart of Darkness*), we have already established a version of his character by the technique of symbolic association. He is established as a man of imagination, talent and value being associated with the visionary painting and the ivory itself.

Test your understanding

Using a text you have read recently, find an example of each technique of characterisation.

See structuralism.

characters

Creations in narratives or dramas that cause the action to progress.

E. M. Forster in *Aspects of the Novel* (1927) thought that there were two kinds of characters—flat and round. Flat characters, he said, tend to be based on a single idea and only receive a limited set of personal qualities. They do not change over the course of the plot. Round characters are more complex and they tend to change as the plot progresses. Round characters have complex motivations, and they can be given detailed and even subtle descriptions.

Another way of thinking about characters is to see them as agents or an element of the narrative that performs a particular function. Some critics have drawn up lists of the different types of agents that can exist in a story. The Russian academic Vladimir Propp suggested that there are only seven character types in the folk tales that he studied:

- the hero (who seeks something)
- the villain (who tries to oppose the actions of the hero)
- the false hero (who seems to offer a quick solution to the problem)
- the princess (a sought-for character)
- the father (who sends the hero on his mission)
- the dispatcher (who makes it possible for the hero to undertake the task)
- the donor/helper (who helps the hero through a difficulty).

Whichever view you adopt, it is important to remember that all characters are constructions, and convey particular values and beliefs about the world. In order to read characters effectively, there are five useful questions that you can ask:

- what are they like?
- how are they constructed? (*see* characterisation)
- what functions do they serve in this text?
- what values and beliefs do they support?
- what kind of readers are they designed to appeal to?

Test your understanding

Using a text you have read recently, choose one of the characters and answer the five questions above, providing examples to support your answers.

choice of detail

***See* selection of detail.**

chorus

A group of dancers and singers often used to comment on the action in the plays of the Ancient Greeks.

The chorus are presented as a uniform group, although they can be led by a chorus leader who takes the role of chief spokesperson. The members of the chorus wear the same large masks that illustrate some aspect of their response to the actions of the play. The masks of blank astonishment worn by the chorus in Peter Hall's 1981 production of *The Oresteia* were a constant reminder to the audience of how these respected members of Agamemnon's kingdom felt about the action.

The chorus is able to comment quite forthrightly, almost as if they are not really present. They deliver a forceful moral point in *Oedipus Rex*:

> Antistrophe 2: Time sees all, and... time, in your despite,
> Disclosed and punished your unnatural marriage...

The chorus can also express powerful emotions. When the blinded Oedipus re-enters, the chorus responds:

> Oh horrible, dreadful sight. More
> dreadful far than any I have yet seen...

However, the chorus is limited to these roles of comment and response. They cannot intervene in the action. In more recent literature a similar function is performed by different characters; for example: the fool in Shakespeare's *King Lear* provides an ironic commentary on Lear's fond actions. In Tennessee Williams' *The Glass Menagerie* and Arthur Miller's *A View from the Bridge* the same device is used to present clearly articulated responses to the action.

cinquain

A five-line stanza of poetry with variable meter and rhyme scheme.

For example:

The puppy bumbled
like a sleepy polar bear
stumbled over the slipper
and rolled into a ball
of struggling furry legs.

(F. Parke)

circumlocution

Using many words when few would do.

This is a common fault in poor writing. 'I think, from my own personal point of view…' and 'At about this point in time…' are examples.

See redundancy.

citation

A way of producing evidence in support of an idea.

In the case of citing texts, there are some strict rules about the way the texts must be set out. One method is to cite short texts (poems, short stories, essays, etc.) in inverted commas and to underline longer texts (novels, films, plays, etc.).

class

The categories into which people of a particular society can be placed, depending on their wealth, status, education, occupation, etc.

In Western cultures this is often a simple three-layered set of categories:

- the aristocracy, the rich, the powerful, the upper class
- the middle class
- the working class, the poor.

None of the groupings will be 'natural' or obvious, they will arise from the unequal distribution of power within that society. Those with most power and opportunity will participate in systems and organisations that reinforce that class structure. They will try to make that structure seem natural, so that they are less likely to be challenged by those who are disadvantaged by it.

Class divisions are, however, not as simple as this makes it sound. Particular individuals may be born into one class and marry into another. Elizabeth Bennet does this in *Pride and Prejudice*. Some may, like Becky Sharpe in *Vanity Fair*, by the force of their personality, cross class boundaries. Some may, like Lady Chatterley, cross class boundaries for their own pleasure. However, all this is done with a sense of bravado, a feeling of breaking out of the normal pattern, and it is usually done at great social peril. So in many ways, these crossings underline the power of the class divisions.

The notion of belonging to a class has very important implications for an individual. It will determine educational and social opportunities. It may influence your choice of marriage partner, who you take on as friends and even the way you speak. It will also affect the kinds of values and beliefs that you hold. The novel *The Collector*, by John Fowles, illustrates this idea.

Student example

Miranda Grey is a young student of art, born into a well-to-do family, with a la-di-da voice. Frederick Clegg, who captures her, is a member of the working class, with a troubled upbringing and little opportunity in his life. Clegg believes that money is power and that by winning the soccer pools he will now be more acceptable to Miranda. Throughout the novel he is disappointed as he discovers that they have different views and values because of the different classes they belong to.

To read a text for class issues, ask these questions:

- who has the power and influence?
- on what basis is the power distributed in the world of the text?
- does the text support the values of private ownership and the accumulation of wealth or some other system?
- how are we invited to view the social structure of the world of the text?
- whose interest does the text serve?

Test your understanding

Using a text you have read recently, answer the five questions above, providing examples to support your answers.

See Marxist criticism.

classic

A work of literature that has 'passed the test of time' and is regarded as being of great value. It has earned a place in the canon.

Modern literary theory challenges this notion by asking who decides when a work can be called a 'classic', and how long does it take to pass the test of time? It rejects the idea that any text can be of the same value to all people because different groups of people live by different values. Is Salman Rushdie's novel *The Satanic Verses* a classic? Some would say so, but there are millions of Muslims who would see it very differently.

See canon.

classicism

A movement in art and literature that idealised and imitated the styles, conventions, themes and values of Roman and Ancient Greek artists and writers.

cliché

A phrase or expression that has been worn out by overuse.

When a sportsperson is asked how they rate their chances in a competition they often give the clichéd response, 'I'll just take it one game at a time'. A common cliché you'll see in the media is 'This is a real bargain!' Alexander Pope, in his 'Essay on Criticism', took his contemporaries to task for using clichés in their poetry and explained how their readers might respond:

> Where'er you find 'the cooling western breeze',
> In the next line it 'whispers through the trees';
> If crystal streams 'with pleasing murmurs creep',
> The reader's threatened (not in vain) with 'sleep'.

climax

The part of a narrative or drama at which the crisis point is reached.

This will be towards the end of most texts, after which the problems raised earlier on can be resolved and the text can end with the sense of having been properly worked out.

Student example

The climax of Homer's *The Odyssey* occurs as Odysseus kills the suitors with the bow that only he can string. All the action of the story has been leading up to this point—his difficult voyage home, learning about his wife's great courage and fidelity, and his need to cleanse his household of the self-interested suitors. The tension rises to this point—if he can kill or cast out the suitors then all these issues can be resolved, and we can focus on the joyous reunion between the king and his wife.

See structure.

clincher

A statement that captures the main idea of an argument.

closure

The process of ending a story.

This is not just a matter of tying up the strands of the plot, of solving the problems posed, or of ending the journey and marrying (or killing) off the characters. It includes a 'sense of an ending' by indicating the preferred outcomes, excluding other possibilities, and therefore proposing a preferred reading of the text.

Student example

John Fowles in *The French Lieutenant's Woman* provides us with a so-called 'happy' Victorian ending where Charles settles down with Ernestina. But, of course, we are not fooled by this for two reasons: there are still a lot of pages to read and this is not the kind of novel it is. Fowles offers us two more endings: one that ends happily for Charles and one unhappily. Even though Fowles seems to offer us an open choice, it is clear enough that we should prefer the unhappy ending because it is the more open, and because its mood fits in with the rest of the text...

Test your understanding

Using a fairy tale or other simple story, explain how the ending has proposed a preferred reading.

codes

Systems of rules used to make meanings in the writing and reading of texts.

For example: some of the rules that govern the way a house is built (and thus form part of a code) are that taps should be in the kitchen, bathroom and laundry; and that all rooms should have at least one door. These types of rules allow us to identify each room and to understand what function that room is going to serve in the whole house. We can make sense of the house by the code used to build it. In the same way, the codes that govern the construction of texts (and the reading of them) help us to make meanings.

One of the most influential modern theorists to shape the way we think about texts is Roland Barthes. He suggested that narrative texts are governed by five key codes:

- the character code—a set of rules that help us build up an idea of an individual in a text
- the plot code—a set of rules that help us connect events and build up patterns in narratives so that we can begin to predict what will happen next
- the suspense code—a set of rules that help us build up expectations and questions about events in narratives; they also assist us in not being too frustrated that our questions are not answered or revealed until the end of the story
- the structural code—a set of rules which organise the text around common oppositions like good/bad, moral/immoral, rich/poor, etc.
- the cultural code—a set of rules and beliefs drawn from the culture or cultures surrounding the text.

Student example

John Donne's poem 'A Valediction: Forbidding Mourning' illustrates the operation of the power structure in a patriarchal culture which attempts to naturalise male views in order for them to escape criticism. Donne's poem was written in the seventeenth century in England where the cultural codes supported male dominance. This is made clear in the language of the text...

A point worth noting is that 'codes' is often coupled with 'conventions' in the phrase 'codes and conventions of a text'. The two notions are not the same. *See* conventions to clarify the differences.

colloquial
In the manner of everyday speech.

A colloquial style is casual, relaxed, neither slang nor formal. Derived from the Latin *co* (together), *loqui* (speak)—it literally means 'speaking together'.
See slang.

comedy
A genre of texts that provokes amusement or laughter through the presentation of human weaknesses.

Because of this, comedies can often have a cruel or distasteful side to them. Satires on fat people or jokes about the Irish may not always meet with approving laughter. (*See* humour.)

The oldest existing form of comedy is the Greek plays of Aristophanes, for example: *The Frogs, Clouds*, and *Lysistrata*. In this context of Ancient Greek drama, comedy is opposed to tragedy. The word is derived from the Greek *komos*, meaning a 'revel' or 'merrymaking'.

Shakespeare's plays have often been divided into tragedies, histories and comedies. The comedies are characterised by characters doing foolish (and sometimes comic) things, leading to, through many complications of the plot, a happy ending, often involving marriage. There are elements of comedy in his tragedies and histories that supply a moment of relief from the tension and drama of the main plot. The porter in *Macbeth* regales us with a comic monologue on the nature of drunkenness just after the murder of Duncan. The fool in *King Lear* provides the king with a satirical and witty set of jibes just after he has been thrown out of his daughters' castles.

More modern types of comedy include the plays of Oscar Wilde, cartoons, American TV sit-coms (situation comedies), stand-up artists like Billy Connelly and Jerry Seinfeld, and a whole genre of films that are grouped under the category of comedy in local video stores.

comedy of manners
A genre that focuses on the social codes and the behaviour of men and women, some of whom do not conform to society's expectations.

Most dramas of this type are preoccupied with the codes of the middle and upper classes. Some famous examples are Shakespeare's *Much Ado About Nothing* and *Love's Labour's Lost*, Oscar Wilde's *The Importance of Being Earnest*, and Noel Coward's *Private Lives*. Many of the British TV comedy shows fit into this genre.

commedia dell'arte
A form of comic drama developed in sixteenth century Italy in which stock characters often improvise dialogue around a basic scenario.

Some of the stock characters were a pair of young lovers, an old man (Pantaloon), a clever and intriguing servant (Harlequin), and a clown or buffoon (Punch).

comparison (and contrast)
To read one text beside another and pick out particular aspects that are similar.

This is the basis of figurative language when one object or idea is described more clearly by comparing it to some other object or idea, for example: 'The way this car runs reminds me of Dad's old tractor'.

Student example

In *Four Weddings and a Funeral* Tom's brand of cheerful idiocy always keeps the atmosphere of the weddings buoyant, and is very similar to James Fleet's role in the British situation comedy 'The Vicar of Dibley'. There he plays Hugo Houghton, an exact replica of Tom in terms of his affable 'twittishness'.

Writers like E. M. Forster and Italo Calvino emphasise the importance of making connections between words, texts or ideas. Calvino writes that at some point in the writing or reading process, the text:

> ...is invested with an unexpected meaning, a meaning that is not patent on the linguistic plane on which we were working but has slipped in from another level, activating something that on the second level is of great concern to the author (or reader) or his society.

Test your understanding

Explain how a comparison (used in a text you have read recently) has provided that fragment of text with an 'unexpected meaning'.

composing
The construction of a text.

Writers will be aware that they compose their texts for a particular audience and that they have a particular purpose in writing it. For example: teachers write reports to parents to explain student progress; and reporters write articles on events to inform people about that event. Writers and readers will also be aware that their text's meanings will arise from the relationship between writers, readers, context and text. This means that the text they write will arise from a complex interaction between the subject; the writer's background and culture; their attitudes and values; and the choices they make about genre, style and structure. The diagram on page 63 illustrates these relationships.

Student example A

This is the opening of a commentary on a narrative composed by the student:

This story has been written by me, drawn from my personal experience, and based on lots of texts that I have read and viewed. The more I thought about it the more I realised that, in some strange way, I didn't actually make the story up all by myself. In fact, I just sort of pulled a whole lot of threads together to make the story different from what I've already read, a kind of patchwork quilt of texts that already exist. For example: the way I characterised Eric 'the popular guy in school' with his sexy jeans and shirt, his soap and after-shave... he sounds like some guy straight out of 'Friends'.

Student example B

Four Weddings and a Funeral is like any other text—it is a complex web of forces bearing social, political, cultural, economic and industrial aspects. It is about a group of wealthy English socialites (most of them twittish) presented to us in a time when we have nearly 10 per cent unemployment.

See author.

comprehending
The process of making meanings from texts.

When reading a text, the meanings arise from the interactions between the writer, the text, the context and the reader. This means that the same text can have different meanings for different readers.

See reading, meaning.

conceit
A figure of speech which sets up a striking comparison between two things which are, at first glance, very different.

The most memorable is perhaps John Donne's comparison of two lovers' souls to two legs of a compass in his poem 'A Valediction: Forbidding Mourning'.

See oxymoron.

conclusion
The final paragraph of an essay.

A good conclusion should draw all the main threads of the argument together, provide a 'clincher' in which the main force of the argument is clear and indicate the significance of the argument in a wider context.

See essay.

concrete poetry
Poetry which asks to be read as a visual whole.

This often means that the shape or layout of the words on the page reflects an aspect of the subject matter. Sometimes the typing or punctuation have been used to disrupt normal reading techniques and challenge the reader to see the poem differently. e e cummings' poem 'r-p-o-p-h-e-s-s-a-g-r' is a fine example. The following poem by F. Hill is an example of how the shape of a poem can add something to our interpretations.

Pa
my
pa
did
not
work
his big
rough hands
would only
tremble and
clench into
fists. When
he returned
it was late
too late my
mother and
me were gone.

confessional literature

Texts which are very personal and provide an account of the writer's or persona's experience, thoughts, feelings and beliefs.

Although the style of confessional literature would lead us to think that the 'confession' is about the writer's life, ideas and feelings it is not necessarily so. Some writers adopt a persona to explore ideas and lives different from their own. Some famous examples are Saint Augustine's *Confessions*, Albert Camus' *The Fall* and some of Sylvia Plath's poetry.

See persona.

conflict

The contest between the protagonist of a story and the opposing forces.

These opposing forces may be: a woman (women), a man (men), God, society, fate, nature or even opposing desires/values in the protagonist's own mind. Identifying the conflicting forces is a useful way to understand the structure of a narrative:

- identify the protagonist(s) and what they desire—what is it they want to achieve?
- identify the opposing forces—what stands in the way of this desire?
- what does the protagonist do to overcome these forces?
- what are the outcomes of the protagonist's actions?

Test your understanding

Using a narrative you have read recently, answer the above questions. Identify the opposing forces.

Does your answer help make the structure of the text clear? If you need more help here, *see* characters.

connotation/denotation

The denotations of a word are its primary meanings, the ones found in the dictionary. The connotations of a word are the associations we make with the word.

For example: 'mouse' denotes a small rodent. However, its connotations may be, for one person, 'loveable pet'; another may see it as 'laboratory specimen'; and yet another may respond with fright regarding 'mouse' as an 'alarming pest'. This is one of the reasons why texts may mean different things to different readers.

Student example

In 'Design' by Robert Frost, he has presented the spider, the moth and the flower as white, and by connotation, pure and clean. Yet he suggests that in the hands of Fate, they become 'the ingredients of witches' broth', revealing a darker side of planned destruction in nature.

Test your understanding

Write connotations and denotations for each of these words:

1 home
2 fire
3 school
4 ocean.

consonance

The repetition of a series of consonants to draw attention to particular words or to create a special effect.

For example: 'She sells sea shells by the sea shore' is an entertaining tongue twister; and 'Slip, slop, slap' has made the rule easier to remember.

See assonance.

construct/construction

Something made by one or more individuals, involving choices.

Often, the term 'construct' is used to refer to a system of thought, for example: science is a construct. Science contains a series of beliefs and assumptions on which all its theory is built. In order to participate in science, a person must accept the basic assumptions, values and ideas of the construct. The same is true of religion, the family, society—even our versions of reality are constructs—they are based on beliefs, assumptions and ideas, all of which are open to challenge.

It is useful to refer to texts as constructs since it draws attention to the fact that writers shape texts in particular contexts for particular audiences to achieve particular purposes. This means that texts are not neutral or objective but always carry with them a set of values, beliefs and opinions that underpin the construction.

See belief.

context

The surrounding circumstances.

The context of an extract from a novel is all the text surrounding it. What has come just before? What happens after? What happens in the rest of the text? How do the extract and the rest of the text affect each other? A text also has a context in its culture, for example: a new Stephen King novel is received with expectations about its genre (horror), its language (fairly simple, colloquial), and its values and attitudes.

Texts are produced and read in particular circumstances. These circumstances affect the way the text is constructed and received. Elizabethan England had a strong impact on Shakespeare's plays—particularly in the portraits of kings and queens of England and how well they were regarded by the Elizabethan court. The society of the time also affected the way these plays were performed; since women were not allowed to be involved in the (immoral) dealings of the theatre then young boys were asked to play the female roles. Some critics claim this is why Shakespeare wrote so few major roles for females—and so many parts for women disguising themselves as men.

The reader's context will also affect the ways texts are read, for example: Vikram Seth's poem 'Biko' which laments the death of Steve Biko the South African described as 'a spokesman for black consciousness' will probably be read differently by black and white South Africans.

Student example

The gender stereotypes in Donne's poem 'Elegie: To his Mistris on Going to Bed' are revealed through the addresser's arrogance, in both his language and his proposed actions. My response to the poem is a negative one; for, being female, I dislike the nature of the patriarchal society in which I live and the one that this poem portrays...

contradictions

Ideas in a text which mean or imply the opposite of what has already been stated.

In the case of irony, the contradiction is highlighted for the reader. We are invited to see the difference between what Jonathan Swift says in 'A Modest Proposal' and what he really means. Few readers would take his invitations to present 'fricassee of baby' seriously. The same is true of sarcasm. When someone is labelled 'God's gift to women!' we know we must read this as a contradiction (*contra*—against; *dicto*—what is said).

There are also contradictions in texts which are only revealed under sharp analysis. These arise from circumstances such as discrepancies between the writer's personal beliefs and those they feel they should hold, or conflicts between what is asserted and what is demonstrated. For example: the Bible asserts; 'Thou shalt not kill', but then praises kings, fathers and others for killing their enemies.

In Shakespeare's *Romeo and Juliet* Romeo says often enough that he loves Juliet—but does he demonstrate that he does or is he just playing out an idealised role? Readers of Daniel Defoe's preface to the 1721 edition of *Moll Flanders* will thoughtfully read his justification for his tale:

> as the best use is to be made even of the worst story, the moral 'tis hoped will keep the reader serious...

Probably, they will see this as being contradicted by the details of the story of Moll who was 'Twelve Year a Whore, five times a Wife (where of once to her own brother)...'.

conventions

Widely accepted techniques or devices that audiences may expect to find in a text of a particular genre.

Conventions are strongly linked with genres. A genre is a set of conventions which gives the author and the reader an agreed structure within which they can both work. It is widely accepted that in a stage drama actors will stand around in a lighted area and talk with each other, while the audience will sit in the dark and not talk. Some conventions are not always so easily accepted, in fact, it is a feature of conventions that they are constantly changing. It was conventional in Victorian and early twentieth century literature (and polite society) to be discreet and indirect about sexual matters. Now it is more conventional to be open and direct about them.

Writers are also apt to challenge the current conventions in their literary works. B. S. Johnson, the novelist, presented his novel *The Unfortunates* as a series of separately bound chapters, in random order, in a box. This worked as a tangible metaphor for randomness and the nature of fate. The normal convention, of course, is to present the chapters in a pre-determined and meaningful order.

Test your understanding
What are the main techniques that are used conventionally in the following genres? An example has been provided for each one.

1 prose fiction (for example, characterisation is used to create imaginary identities who embody particular values and attitudes)
2 drama (for example, lighting is used to represent different times of the day)
3 poetry (for example, rhyme is used to create links between one line or one word and another).

conventions of drama

Conventions are a set of widely accepted techniques or devices that audiences may expect to find in a drama.

All of the conventions are too numerous to list here, but a selection follows:

- the stage will be separate from the audience
- it will be brightly lit
- things that happen there will only be a pretence (that is, if someone is shot we should not call the police).

Some of the conventions of dialogue used in a play are:

- the aside—we must believe that no-one else heard what was said, even though *we* did
- the soliloquy—the character is revealing her thoughts to us, not showing signs of mental instability.

Whatever the conventions used by a particular text they will always be changing and open to challenge by the next generation of writers.
See conventions.

conventions of film

Conventions are a set of widely accepted techniques and devices that audiences may expect to find in a film.

Some of the techniques that can be used conventionally in a feature film are plot, character, setting, dialogue, action, lighting, costume, camera positioning and music. Some of the main conventions of a feature film connected with the plot are:

- there is one main plot, although there may be several sub-plots
- flashbacks in time can be used to reveal the past
- the film can show us what is happening in several places at once
- the end of the plot will tie up most of the strands and the film will soon end.

Some of the techniques that can be used conventionally in a documentary film are interviews, dramatic reconstructions, voice-over, library footage, camera positioning, music and on-the-spot reporting.
See conventions.

conventions of narrative

Conventions are a set of widely accepted techniques and devices that audiences may expect to find in a novel, short story or other narrative.

Some of the techniques that are used conventionally are plot, character, setting, point of view, diction and dialogue. Some of the conventions associated with point of view are:

- if one character is telling the story they can only tell what they could reasonably be expected to know
- if a third person's point of view is being used they can tell what is going on in two places at once, they can present the thoughts of any character at any time.

conventions of poetry

Conventions are a set of widely accepted techniques and devices that audiences may expect to find in a poem.

Some of the techniques that are used conventionally are form, sound devices, imagery, persona and diction. For example: it is conventional for the sonnet form to have fourteen lines and a tight rhyme scheme.
See conventions.

couplet

A pair of successive rhyming lines.

Some poems can be written entirely in couplets, as the poetry of Chaucer, the Elizabethans and Alexander Pope. Many sonnets end with a couplet to provide that sense of an ending—a final emphatic statement on the subject as seen here in Shakespeare's Sonnet 130:

And yet by heaven I think my love as rare
As any she belied with false compere.

critical analysis

The detailed interpretation and evaluation of a text, including aspects of the reader's and the writer's context, as well as the construction and content of the text itself.

Before the eighteenth century, criticism tended to focus on how well a text imitated the texts of Ancient Greece and Rome (called 'the classical tradition'). Since then, many literary theories have blossomed. In the middle of the twentieth century, F. R. Leavis and the other writers grouped under the title 'new criticism' argued that texts (poems, in particular) should be read as a separate and isolated object, and that readers should focus on the content and construction of that text only. In this way, it was thought, the critical analysis could be objective and readers would discover the 'true meaning' of the text.

In the latter half of the twentieth century, literary critics rejected this idea in favour of a wide variety of reading practices. Rather than seeing texts as reflecting reality and containing universal truths that readers had to work out by close reading, postmodern literary theory suggests that whatever reading practice you use, the meaning you come up with will be (as in all other social practices) a product of the struggle for meaning and power between different sets of beliefs and values. So feminist readers may focus on the way texts represent women. Marxist readers may be concerned with the way texts deal with the distribution of power between workers and bosses, etc. In other words, the critical analysis of a text will involve aspects of the reader's and writer's context as well as dealing with the text and its construction—and different readers may produce widely varying readings. The following student example shows how the reader's context has influenced their response to the text.

Student example

The poem 'Ala' by Grace Nichols deals with the abuse and humiliation black slaves suffered in the early eighteenth century. Even though Nichols is probably referring to her native Guyana, the images in 'Ala' remind me of some of the scenes of torture and brutality from *Uncle Tom's Cabin*...

This essay continued by analysing the way the images of brutality positioned him as a white reader.

critical approaches (meaning systems)

A systematic way of reading texts, based on the reader's beliefs and practices as a member of a cultural group.

There are many very influential ways of thinking that may affect an individual reader's approach to reading. Some of these are:

- Christianity—provides a set of beliefs and assumptions for readers based on the Bible and other religious teachings, for example: The Ten Commandments
- feminism—provides a set of beliefs and assumptions for readers based on modern feminist thought, for example: that patriarchal culture attempts to naturalise the power of men and the marginalisation of women
- Marxism—provides a set of beliefs and assumptions for readers based on the philosophies of Karl Marx and other Marxist thinkers, for example: that society's classes will always struggle against each other for power and wealth.

critical literacy

The ability to demonstrate through reading, viewing, writing, speaking and listening understandings, that language is a dynamic social process which responds to and reflects changing social conditions.

Critical literacy demands an awareness that in using English we are involved in creating and restructuring values, beliefs and ways of thinking about the world and ourselves, and that the meanings we construct are dependent on context, purpose and audience. It also demands that we develop an appreciation and sensitivity to sociocultural diversity. Critical literacy depends on functional literacy*.

* This definition is a paraphrase of the definition of critical literacy found in the Western Australian Curriculum Council's *Curriculum Framework for Kindergarten to Year 12 Education in Western Australia* (1998).

critical objectivity

The evaluation and interpretation of texts without bias or undue influence from other sources.

Critics taking this approach reject the influences of the writers, readers and their worlds on the text and the meanings created. They see the literary text as a self-sufficient object to be judged by 'intrinsic' and 'objective' criteria. Recent critics have rejected these ideas since, they say, all texts are part of a cultural fabric that can only be properly read in context.

criticism

The interpretation and evaluation of texts.

See critical analysis.

critique

An essay or article for publication in a magazine or newspaper that interprets and evaluates a particular text. The text could be a novel, poem, play, film or even CD.

See critical analysis.

cultural identity

A way of distinguishing one culture from another by defining their practices, beliefs and values.

No culture is uniform, so this notion will always be confined to particular groups—usually the dominant group within the culture. Other groups might be ignored. Cultures are always changing and an identity that may have applied last century might not be applicable now. Australians, for example, might have seen themselves as 'bronzed diggers, battling a tough land'. Today, that image seems old fashioned, and perhaps, 'a multicultural nation trying to save a degraded environment' might be closer to the mark. Whatever cultural identity is proposed for a particular culture, it will always carry with it a set of beliefs and values. This is why the notion is important in the study of literature.

Student example

In Seamus Heaney's 'The Toome Road' we see an expression of cultural identity from the point of view of the suppressed Catholic minority in Northern Ireland... One of the most important and defining aspects of Heaney's work is his rejection of the English and English values... he sees them as the latest in a long line of invaders and we appreciate the resentment he feels:

> How long were they approaching down
> my roads
> As if they owned them?

cultural myth

A myth is a story by which a culture explains or understands some aspect of nature or itself.

The Ancient Greek myths explain such things as how the seasons began. The story of Persephone and Demeter does this:

> Once it was always warm and the land was always fruitful. One day Hades, the King of the Underworld, captured Demeter's daughter, Persephone and took her to be his bride. Demeter, the Earth Goddess, mourned for her daughter and neglected the land. Winter began.

This story sounds strange to us, but it was no doubt a comforting explanation to the Ancient Greeks. Possibly, the myths or stories we tell ourselves in the twentieth century will sound equally strange to people in a few thousand years time.

The myths told in our culture explain aspects of our experience. One of our modern myths is that 'science helps us control nature'. We see this story every week on TV and in the newspapers—'a new drug to fight AIDS', 'better weather satellites help farmers'. But the counter myth is also present. It is widely thought that science exploits nature and shows our lack of understanding—'our modern technologies create terrible pollution'. An understanding of the myths that a text presents will be a valuable key to deconstructing the values and assumptions made in that text.

See ideology.

culture

There are two definitions to consider:

- activities and beliefs that are considered to be in good taste in a society
- the values, beliefs and practices of a particular group of people.

Culture is often opposed to nature. This can be a useful binary opposition to deconstruct a text.

Note that cultures are constantly changing and that individuals can move in and out of certain cultures. For example: a young man who was a bikie for ten years might join the priesthood. Large groups of people (for example, 'Australian culture') will be diverse in their values, beliefs and practices, so it is difficult to say anything that applies to all people in Australian culture.

culture and nature

A binary opposition that can be used to locate the beliefs, values and assumptions in a text.

> **Student example**
> The car advertisement presents some opening shots of the two people in the car in a high-rise city—the pinnacle of culture. This setting is complex, stressful and confining. The negative aspects of culture are emphasised. When the car breaks through the paper facade of a building to race free on a country road, we see the people are getting back to nature, breaking free, and having fun. The car becomes a symbol of empowerment...

current affairs TV

Short, documentary-style reports on items of popular, topical interest.

Current affairs programs often present items of human interest and strongly position viewers in relation to the subject matter. All TV news and current affairs programs present viewers with a particular version of reality that is based on certain values, beliefs and assumptions. Viewers should be aware that these reports are not objective; some might even be biased.

> **Student example**
> In the 1999 Kosovo conflict CNN and the BBC news reported that a convoy of refugees was strafed by a Yugoslav Airforce fighter jet. Serbian TV reported that it was a NATO plane. Such conflicting reports in our TV news and current affairs programs undermine our confidence in our news sources...

Current affairs TV programs differ from documentaries in length, the detail and rigour which they apply, and the methods they use to position viewers.

See documentary.

Dd

Dadaism

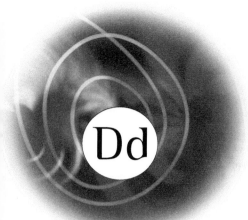

A movement in art that rejected all the rules and restrictions of the nineteenth century.

Dadaism was popular in France after the First World War. Its influence is evident in the poetry of T. S. Eliot and Ezra Pound.

deconstruction

A form of criticism that focuses on the different possible readings of texts and the contradictions between them.

It demonstrates that any preference for one reading or meaning above the others is always based on beliefs and assumptions, and not something inherent in the words on the page. The following questions are one possible way of generating multiple meanings from texts, and exposing some of their assumptions and beliefs. The student responses are based on the following text:

All fruit
reduced this
week.

- What genre is this text? What do I know about texts composed in this genre?
  Answer: It is an advertisement in a store—trying to entice us to buy. Most advertisements make doubtful promises.
- What is the subject/theme/issue?
  Answer: It says the fruit is cheaper this week.
- What is left out? Why? What does this mean about the things omitted?
  Answer: Is the fruit any good? Is it of worse quality than last week? Why is it cheaper? Were last week's prices too high? How much is it reduced by?
- How are readers positioned to see all these things (both those included and excluded)?
  Answer: The shopkeeper hopes we will think this is a 'bargain' price and buy lots of fruit.
- What techniques are used to position readers in relation to the subject/s?
  Answer: The fact that it is only 'this week' suggests we should hurry.
- Who has made this text? Who is speaking? What kind of audience is the text expecting? Who is privileged by the text? Who is marginalised? Why?
  Answer: The shopkeeper made the sign to boost selling—expecting weekly shoppers and hoping they will buy more fruit this week. Perhaps hoping to attract shoppers who normally buy their fruit elsewhere.
- What are the assumptions of the text?
  Answer: The text assumes many things: we know 'reduced' means price, not quality or size; and that the price will go up again next week.
- Are there other possible readings of the text?
  Answer: Which week? This calendar week? Or, a week after the sign went up? All fruit? Does this include tomatoes (which are really a fruit)? Are the prices usually too high?
- What version of reality are we invited to endorse?
  Answer: That the shopkeeper is being nice to customers and giving them a bargain. But this reading ignores the problems above.
- What is your preferred reading? Why?
  Answer: I prefer the reading made in the answer to point 6 and that the shopkeeper could keep fruit prices down all the time—if they wanted to.

Test your understanding
Using a text you have read recently, find answers to these ten points and provide specific examples to support your answers.

defamiliarisation

A technique that helps us to see familiar things in a new light—to make them seem 'strange' again.

Writers can do this in literary works by using devices like imagery or allegory. W. B. Yeats does this in 'Sailing to Byzantium' when he describes an old man:

> An aged man is but a paltry thing,
> A tattered coat upon a stick...

Critics can use this technique to expose beliefs and assumptions in texts when they deconstruct the text.

See deconstruction.

denotation

The commonly accepted meaning of a word, as described in a dictionary.

See connotation/denotation.

denouement

The resolution of the plot's complications. The word comes from French, meaning 'unknotting'.

See resolution.

descriptive language

A loose term, often used to label language that creates a vivid picture of an object or scene.

Students may be better advised to consider diction or imagery. They may also be better advised to consider the nature and effect of the diction or imagery, rather than label a text as having 'lots of descriptive language'.

Gershon Legman wrote:

> Murder is a crime. Describing murder is not.
> Sex is not a crime. Describing sex is.

deus ex machina

An artificial and unanticipated way of solving the problems and complications of the plot of a narrative or drama.

The term comes from the Latin and literally means 'god out of the machine'. This phrase refers to the practice in Ancient Greek drama of lowering a god onto the stage (by a machine) so that they could help the hero overcome difficulties and untangle the problems raised in the plot. Euripides used the device often. Now the phrase is applied to any unanticipated (and unsatisfactory) way of overcoming a difficult situation in a plot.

dialogue

Speech between characters in a narrative or drama.

The dialogue is thought to reveal characters' thoughts, feelings, motivations, prejudices and fears. It also advances the plot.

diary

A personal, usually private, daily record of events, feelings and thoughts.

Ellen Terry wrote of diaries:

> What is a diary as a rule? A document useful to the person who keeps it, dull to the contemporary who reads it, invaluable to the student centuries afterwards, who treasures it!

Some of the best known diaries are the diary of Samuel Pepys (1633–1703), *Diary of a Nobody* by George and Weedon Grossmith (1894), *In Search of a Character* by Graham Greene (1962) and *Go Ask Alice* by an anonymous writer. The diary is often used as a literary form for the presentation of a narrative, for example: *The Secret Diary of Adrian Mole* by Sue Townsend and *Gulliver's Travels* by Jonathan Swift.

diatribe

A stinging attack on a thing or person couched in cutting or even abusive language.

diction

The choice of words, phrases or images in a text.

The diction of a text can be taken from common speech or from some more specialised vocabulary. It may represent the language of a special group or a social class.

Student example

In D. H. Lawrence's poem 'Snake' the persona is confronted by a long golden snake drinking water at his trough. His reaction to the snake is double-sided. He is afraid of it and he admires it. This is conveyed in the diction. Phrases like 'that horrid black hole', 'slack long body' and 'from the burning bowels of the earth' give voice to that fear...

diegetic effect

The compelling effect on a viewer or reader which causes them to suspend their disbelief and become involved in the 'reality' offered by the text.

This term is most often used in connection with film, but can also apply to other text types. Narrative is one of the most powerful elements that can produce a diegetic effect, but diegesis can occur without strong narrative.

See suspension of disbelief.

digression

Ideas or material not directly relevant to the main thread of an argument or narrative.

direct speech

The speech of characters in a narrative presented directly.

Direct speech is usually easily identified by the use of inverted commas to separate what the character has said from the rest of the narrative. The alternative is reported speech in which case the narrator explains what the character said and thus there is no need to use inverted commas. Direct speech is usually more dramatic because it provides the impression that it is more immediate.

discourse

A way of speaking or writing used by a particular group, related to their social position and practices.

For example: doctors will speak about their patients using a medical discourse; scientists will argue about theories in a scientific discourse; and feminists will analyse texts using a feminist discourse. The discourse used by an individual helps to shape their attitudes, beliefs and behaviours, and influences the power they hold in relation to other people. In every case, there are situations where some people can use the discourse and thereby have power over those who cannot.

Student example

In response to John Donne's poem 'Elegie: To his Mistris Going to Bed'.

The addresser uses a male, sexist discourse to assume the dominant role in the relationship. Telling her 'off with that girdle' so that her 'beauteous state' is revealed, implies that the woman is an object of the man's desire, and that her role is to reveal herself to please the man.

Test your understanding

Describe the users and the discourse that include these terms:

1 blitz, out-flank, division, tactics
2 controlled crying, childproof, tummy time, baby-safe
3 depression, front, isobars, barometric pressure

docudrama

A fictionalised film version of real events.

documentary

A film that deals with actual events, issues and characters.

To document is to put something on record—to organise information about a subject. However, documentaries can never be objective. They will always present a particular view of the subject or issue through the processes of selection and emphasis. John Grierson called his film documentaries 'a creative interpretation of reality'.

Some of the main types of documentaries are travelogues, nature records, social issues, political issues and historical accounts.

Student example

The documentary *The Panama Deception* argues that the USA illegally invaded Panama for selfish reasons. It characterised the Panamanians as innocent, friendly, fun-loving people who became the victims of American greed. The Americans are portrayed as sophisticated, devious and aggressive...

doggerel

A term used to describe rough, ill-crafted verse.

It usually has a regular rhythm that quickly makes it sound monotonous as in the following example by John G. Saxe:

'I can't describe the wedding-day,
Which fell in the lovely month of May,
Nor stop to tell of the honeymoon,
And how it vanished all too soon...'

dominant readings

A dominant reading is one that is produced by a majority of readers in a particular culture at a particular time.

It represents the views and beliefs that are most powerful in the culture at that time. It could be said that these are readings which the text appears to invite. Readers who produce dominant readings claim to be using the same rules as the text, making most of the same assumptions as the text.

Dominant readings tend to make themselves look like the 'common sense' approach to the text. That is, their assumptions and beliefs fit in very neatly with the most widely accepted assumptions and beliefs in that culture. They are said to naturalise themselves.

Different readers will produce different readings of the same text depending on such factors as their education, their cultural context, and their preferred system of values and beliefs. For example, here are four different student responses to a McDonald's TV advertisement.

Student example A
This is a really cool ad. Maccas really know how to appeal to kids our age by using 'The Simpsons' to promote their food. I like the music too. And the burgers look pretty appetising.

Student example B
This ad reminds me of how unhealthy this kind of food is. The burgers are presented as being good to eat, and the fries look clean and crisp but I know that all fast food chains work on two principles—use lots of salt to enhance any flavour the food might have and use lots of fat so that it slides down easily. Yuk!

Student example C
I know the girl in this ad—Peta. She works at Maccas in the city. She was a good choice for the ad as she's pretty good looking and always smiling. She's the kind of person that makes you think you should run in to get a burger just to be served by her.

Student example D
I hate looking at this ad as I've read that companies like this one are responsible for cutting down hectares of forest every day just to supply the packaging for their products.

Test your understanding
Which of the student readings are dominant readings? Which are alternative readings? Which are resistant readings?

double entendre

A double meaning.

In many cases, one of these meanings is bawdy or rude. For example: in act 1, scene 1 of *Romeo and Juliet* Sampson jokes with Gregory and explains his double entendre ('maiden-head' means hymen):

Sampson: I will be civil with the maids—I will cut off their heads.
Gregory: The heads of the maids?
Sampson: Ay, the heads of the maids or their maiden-heads. Take it in what sense thou wilt.

drama

A performance that occurs in a theatre, with actors taking the parts of characters and performing actions before an audience.

The audience watch the play and willingly suspend their disbelief, becoming caught up in the tensions and emotions of the plot. Each performance is unique.

Drama originated in Ancient Greece where the annual religious festivals often included performances of devotions by actors. These developed into the tragedies and comedies of the famous dramatists such as Euripedes, Aeschylus, Sophocles and Aristophanes.

dramatic conventions

A set of accepted practices and techniques used in drama to create the make-believe of the stage.

Audiences know the rules of these practices and techniques so that when an actor falls on his sword and blood spills onto the stage we do not rush to his aid. Instead, we willingly suspend our disbelief and accept that this representation is Brutus or Othello in his last minutes.

Some of the conventions that have gained widespread acceptance:

- the absence of the fourth wall—the three walls (or parts of) represent the whole room
- the use of conventional dialogue, for example: Julius Caesar speaks English and in iambic pentameter (it is interesting to note that although iambic pentameter reflects the natural rhythms of everyday speech, the content itself is highly conventional, nothing like the hesitant, rambling prosaic language that we speak)

- the manipulation of time—scenes or acts that may take less than an hour may represent the passage of some weeks or even years. Breaks of less than a minute between scenes may represent the passage of many hours
- the transition from one location to another—we easily accept that the stage in scene 1 represents a market place and, without much alteration, represents a room in a house in scene 2.

dramatic irony

A context or a circumstance in a play or narrative where the audience or readers know more than one of the characters does, which leads to that character doing or saying something terribly inappropriate.

The character, of course, thinks their speech or action is appropriate, not knowing the full context. This fills the audience with a sense of dread of what they know will happen because of the character's inappropriate actions or speech (in a tragedy) or sets up a scene for hilarious outcomes (in a comedy). In *Oedipus Rex*, a tragic irony occurs when the king, Oedipus, sets out to hunt down the previous king's killer. The audience knows (or has a growing understanding) that it is Oedipus himself who is the killer, so his many proclamations to hunt down and to severely punish the killer serve to reinforce the irony and ensure that he is locked into his tragic fate.

Shakespeare's *King Lear* involves a sustained irony in which the old king is plagued for most of the action of the play by his foolish decision to give his kingdom away to two of his three daughters on the basis of how well they say they love him. The youngest, Cordelia, says nothing (refusing to play the game) and is exiled. The audience understands that real love is bigger than words and that the only daughter to show her love to her father is the one he has cast away.

A structural irony occurs when a structural feature is used to sustain two different levels of meaning. The naive narrator is a common technique used to create one version of events that the knowing audience re-interprets. Huckleberry Finn is a naive narrator in *The Adventures of Huckleberry Finn* by Mark Twain. He does not recognise the selfish motives of the characters he meets, but the readers do, and that creates an entertaining and often amusing tension between Huck's versions of events and the reader's more worldly-wise versions.

dramatic monologue

A form of poetry in which the persona (who is not the poet) delivers an address to a silent listener at an important point in their lives. In doing this they reveal significant aspects of their character.

Robert Browning's 'My Last Duchess', 'The Bishop Orders His Tomb' and 'Porphyria's Lover' are among the best examples. Tennyson's 'Ulysses' and T. S. Eliot's 'The Love Song of J. Alfred Prufrock' are also notable examples.

dramatisation

Turning a text into a dramatic production (a play, film or TV series).

The text may be a script, a novel or a news story, but the final product will use the dramatic or filmic conventions. Film versions of novels are often regarded as a disappointment because they are unable, within about two hours, to recreate the depth of character and the subtlety of plotting created in the novel. The BBC TV mini-series *Pride and Prejudice* (1996) is a fine example of a successful dramatisation of a novel.

Shakespeare's histories like *Richard III* and *Henry IV* can be seen as dramatisations of history, and documentaries of modern history can also contain dramatisations or re-creations of past events, although the entire documentary is not to be classified as a dramatisation.

See docudrama, documentary.

dumb show

An episode in a spoken play that is played out without words.

The actions are therefore open to a range of interpretations. It was a common device in Elizabethan drama. The most famous is the dumb show in *Hamlet*, the play-within-the-play called, by Prince Hamlet, 'The Mousetrap'. It shows an ancient story in which a king is poisoned by his jealous brother. The content, Hamlet hoped, would trigger a guilty reaction in King Claudius.

Ee

elegy

A poem that laments the death of a relative, friend or famous figure.

Some well-known modern elegies are 'Elegy Written in a Country Churchyard' by Thomas Gray, 'In Memoriam' by Tennyson and 'Elegy for Drowned Children' by Bruce Dawe.

An elegy is written in elegiac meter (alternative hexameter and pentameter lines) and addresses serious subjects and issues such as love or bereavement.

Elizabethan period

The time surrounding the reign of Queen Elizabeth I of England, 1558–1603.

This was a period of prosperity and expansion of English trade and power. It was during Elizabeth's reign that the East Indies, West Indies and the New World were opened up for trading. Tobacco, potatoes and other exotic products were introduced to English homes. The Spanish Armada, sent to invade England, was defeated.

Elizabeth's court was a colourful one, full of intrigue and gossip. It was also a colourful time in literature and the arts. Many of the writers and artists are still studied today, for example: Shakespeare, Marlowe, Spenser, Raleigh, Bacon, Ben Jonson and others.

ellipsis

The omission of one or more words in a sentence, indicated by the use of three consecutive dots or stops.

This is often used when quoting another text to cut down the length of the quote. The ellipsis is necessary to indicate that some of the original text has been left out.

emotive language

Words or phrases that evoke an emotional response and strongly position readers in relation to a subject.

The opposite is 'referential language' which is a term not widely used nowadays, meaning 'words that are justified by their truth'.

Student example

Hal Crawford, the reporter, writes about an air crash in his article 'Visit to Crash Site Reveals Images of Hell'. He uses very emotive language to describe the bodies at the site—'missing heads, contorted or severed limbs, exposed bones' and 'The stench of burning flesh'. This is to shock us...

Test your understanding

What is the effect of the following examples of emotive language?

1 This latest concocted idea is a slimy way of getting rid of all the older members.

2 That dog is a vicious killer—it should be put down.

3 He's a loose cannon and he'll destroy all our plans if we let him.

See connotation/denotation, objective/subjective.

empathy

The involuntary association of a reader with a character or object in a text causing a physical reaction in the reader.

For example, a reader may experience a slight flexing of the neck and shoulders when they read Shakespeare's lines from *Venus and Adonis*:

> ...the snail, whose tender horns being hit,
> Shrinks backwards in his shelly cave with
> pain...

Or, perhaps, viewers of the film *Saving Private Ryan* (Spielberg, 1998) may have found themselves flinching or even ducking for cover in the Normandy beach landing scenes.

emphasis

Stress laid upon and importance given to a word or phrase in a sentence or paragraph.

In texts this can be indicated by placing the words to be emphasised in bold or italic type.

Test your understanding

Explain the different interpretations invited by the different emphases.

1 **Year eight** students may go to the swimming carnival.
2 Year eight students may go to the **swimming** carnival.
3 Year eight students **may** go to the swimming carnival.

endings

See **closure.**

English language

The words used by English speakers and the rules governing their usage.

There are more than 600 000 words in the longest English dictionaries. The furthest back we can trace the development of English is to the language spoken by the people who lived around the Baltic sea about 5 000 years ago. That language is called a Proto-Indo-European language or PIE. From this language nearly all the European and East Asian languages were developed as these people migrated south and east.

English has had major influences from the Celts, Greeks, Romans, Angles, Saxons and Jutes, Germans, and French. As with any language it continues to change every day as words are added or fall into disuse. The changes the English language has gone through are divided into three periods:

- Old English—which resembled Modern German more closely than Modern English.
- Middle English—in the period after the Norman invasion (1066) the influence of the Normans (from France) was so significant that French was the language used at court and in business and trade for many years. By the end of the fourteenth century intermarriage and political and cultural influences saw English once again established as the official language of England.
- Modern English—by 1500 English had come to resemble the version we speak today. The invention of printing, the spread of new learning and the rise of the London version of English were three important influences on the form of English that gained widespread acceptance. The printing of the King James Bible in one particular version of English had a powerful influence on which of the four main dialects eventually became the official version. Today, the language continues to change as new words are invented from new fields of technology and new ways of thinking.

English in the early twentieth century was accepted as the international language of science and diplomacy. Perhaps due to the dominance of America in the later part of the twentieth century, English has become accepted as the international language in all areas—especially in tourism, business and politics.

enjambement

Run-on lines in a poem.

Enjambement is taken from the French, literally meaning 'a striding-over'. In traditional forms of verse, many of the lines are end-stopped with a pause mark such as a dash, a comma or even a full stop. Enjambement occurs when the sense of the line carries on to the next line without a pause.

Enlightenment
A period in European history in the seventeenth and eighteenth centuries characterised by the conviction that right-reasoning could find true knowledge and lead humankind to a glorious future.

Many of these scholars looked back to Ancient Greece and Rome for guidance. They found there the inspiration and patterns for a rational and moral order based on proper thought and reason. The literature of the period was very much concerned with the social and moral order. Jonathan Swift's and John Dryden's work showed an underlying insecurity, as if they thought their country's society might fall apart at any moment. Alexander Pope and Dr Samuel Johnson who dominated the latter part of the period were still free in their criticism and satire of their own culture, but they appear to have found more confidence in the stability of English society.

epic
A long narrative poem composed in a serious, elevated style that relates the exploits of a hero, or semi-divine figure from myth, legend or history.

Epics gain their sense of importance from the fact that the fate of a tribe, nation or the human race depends on the success of the central hero. In recent times the term has come to include epic novels and films as well. Some famous examples include Homer's *The Iliad* and *The Odyssey*, the Anglo-Saxon epic *Beowulf*, Tolstoy's *War and Peace*, and Stanley Kubrick's *2001—A Space Odyssey*.

epigram
A short statement in prose or verse, containing wit, and often humour.

Coleridge defined an epigram as:

A dwarfish whole,
Its body brevity, and wit its soul.

Shakespeare's observation 'Youth is wasted on the young' is an epigram that the elderly may find humorous. 'God made women beautiful so men would love them; and he made them stupid so that they could love men'—attributed to La Belle Otero a nineteenth century courtesan. Oscar Wilde's epigrams are well known; for example: 'Work is the curse of the drinking class' and 'I can resist everything except temptation'.

epigraph
An inscription in stone or on a coin or at the head of a chapter.

epilogue
The concluding section of a literary text.

In a play, this is often addressed to the audience. Puck's address at the end of *A Midsummer Night's Dream* is memorable:

If we shadows have offended,
Think but this, and all is mended:
That you have but slumbered here
While these visions did appear...

epitaph
Words to be inscribed on a tomb or headstone.

W. B. Yeats's epitaph reads:

Cast a cold eye
On life, on death.
Horseman, pass by!

epithet
A name or title used to describe some characteristics of a person, for example: Vlad *the Impaler*, Mack *the Knife* or William *the Conqueror*.

epode
A song or chant delivered by the chorus (while standing still) in an Ancient Greek drama.

essay
A prose text of any length that discusses an issue or topic, often presenting a reasoned argument in favour of one particular perspective.

There have been some exceptions written in verse such as Alexander Pope's *Moral Essays*. The word was coined by the French writer Montaigne who called his first publication *Essais* (meaning 'attempts' in French).

The form became very popular in England in the seventeenth century. Some of the best essayists of the time, like Sir Francis Bacon and Joseph Addison are still read as the best examples of the form. Their essays are characterised by their stylishness and wit.

In Addison's essay published in the *Spectator* on 15 January 1712, entitled 'Dissection of a Beau's

Head' (a 'beau' was a young man who engaged in courtly romances and intrigues) he wrote that upon opening up the head of a deceased beau:

> we made a very odd discovery, namely, that what we looked upon as brains, were not such in reality, but a heap of strange materials wound up in that shape and texture...

In more recent times, the writers of the essay like Charles Lamb, Orwell, Thurber and De Quincey have followed Addison's example and published their work in magazines which has brought their work to wider audiences.

A useful distinction can be drawn between the formal and the informal essay. The formal essay is usually impersonal, logically structured and the author claims authority on the issue. The informal essay is more personal in tone (the author develops a voice) and is often whimsical, self-revelatory and sometimes digressions are allowed. The school or academic essay falls between these two types. In an essay you might write for an English, a Literature or a History exam, you will probably be required to do the following:

- answer the question
- provide a logical argument
- provide evidence from texts
- explain how that evidence supports your argument
- write in a tightly structured sequence of thoughts, including an introduction, a thesis statement, paragraphs and a conclusion.

See argument, evidence.

eulogy

A speech or text in praise of a person or thing.

A recent memorable example is Matthew's funeral eulogy in praise of Gareth in the film *Four Weddings and a Funeral*. That moving speech included W. H. Auden's poem 'Stop all the clocks'.

euphemism

A phrase or word substituted for one which is considered tasteless or too blunt.

'To pass away' is a euphemism for 'to die'. Several politically correct terms may fall into this category; for example: 'vertically challenged' is a euphemism for 'short'. Cecily in Oscar Wilde's play *The Importance of Being Earnest* is proud to say that she will not use euphemisms:

> **Cecily:** When I see a spade I call it a spade.

But is undercut by the haughty Gwendolen:

> **Gwendolen:** I am glad to say that I have never seen a spade. It is obvious that our social spheres have been widely different.

Test your understanding

What are the following euphemisms referring to?

1 May I go to the bathroom?
2 She is a lady of the oldest profession.
3 Relatives may see the loved one in the funeral parlour.

What subjects do you think will attract the most euphemisms? Why?

evidence

Material provided in support of an idea or argument.

In an essay, it is essential to provide evidence in support of your ideas—otherwise they remain as unsubstantiated notions. There are two ways of referring to texts to provide evidence—by quoting directly or by referring to a section of the text and paraphrasing its content.

See quotation, paraphrase.

existential philosophy

A view that sees life as possessing no inherent meaning, value or truth.

According to existentialism, we come from nothing and end as nothing, and in between is a brief existence which is filled with anguish. As Samuel Beckett wrote in *Waiting for Godot*:

> They give birth astride a grave,
> the light gleams an instant,
> then it's night once more.

This philosophy arose from the despair felt after the First World War in which too many people died and too much was lost for no human gain. It underpins the novels of Camus and Sartre, and the plays of Genet, Beckett and Stoppard to name a few.

See absurdism.

explication of texts
Producing interpretations of a text.

As with all reading, the interpretations will arise from the relationships between the text, the writer, the reader and their contexts.

exposition
The opening sections of a play or narrative in which the characters and settings are introduced, and the main elements of the plot are established.

It is often difficult to decide where the exposition of a text finishes and the next section, the complication, begins. However, this is perhaps less important than recognising the functions that these two sections perform in the overall narrative structure. The exposition will usually set out the main problem to be solved or overcome by the protagonist; it may also set up events to be worked out in sub-plots.

expository text
A print text that discusses and explains an issue or topic, and provides information on that subject.

Many expository texts claim authority on their subject matter and invite the reader to see their treatment of that subject as unbiased, objective or neutral. Although texts may adopt a style that appears even-handed, no text can be perfectly objective, since all texts embody particular assumptions and carry with them specific values and attitudes, even if they are unnoticed by the writer and reader.

Student example

The article 'Killing Daniel' (Helen Garner) is a shocking and provocative expository text. It challenges the actions of both father and mother as well as the neglect of people in authority. The strong moral voice of the text assumes everyone is guilty until proven innocent...

expressionism
A movement in literature and art that rejects realistic depictions of the world in favour of an expression of the artist's visionary or emotional state of mind.

Edvard Munch's lithograph 'The Scream' epitomises this idea:

fable

A very short story that demonstrates a moral idea or a principle of human behaviour.

The story usually concludes with the narrator or one of the characters expressing the moral in the form of an epigram. The most famous fables, those of Aesop and La Fontaine, use animals for characters. Recent films such as *A Bug's Life* are an extension of this form.

faction

Novels or short stories based on documentary facts. The word is a combination of 'fiction' and 'fact'.

fairy tale

A short story, often passed on in the oral tradition, about good versus evil, and set in a fantasy world.

The characters of fairy tales do include fairies, but also giants, witches, princes and princesses, dragons, dwarves, and animals that talk. There is often an innocent child figure with whom the reader is invited to associate as is the case with *Cinderella* and *Little Red Riding Hood*.

It has been suggested that fairy tales are heavily responsible for passing on the values and rules of our culture to the next generation. For example: princes save princesses from ugly dragons and marry them; father figures save young girls from wolves and order is restored. These models have been challenged by modern writers (especially feminists) and alternative ones have been presented as 'modern fairy tales', for example: the illustrated tales of *Princess Cinders* and *The Paperbag Princess*. Margaret Atwood has written many challenging alternative versions of well-known fairy tales—versions that invite very different readings of the original texts. In 'The Little Red Hen Tells All' from *Good Bones* she writes:

> You know my story. Probably you had it told to you as a shining example of how you yourself ought to behave. Sobriety and elbow-grease. Do it yourself. Then invest your capital. Then collect. I'm supposed to be an illustration of *that*? Don't make me laugh.

fallacy

An error arising from faulty reasoning.

Some of the most common fallacies you may find illustrated in the letters pages of newspapers 'Argumentum ad hominem' (argument against the man) is a technique of discrediting an idea by attacking the character of the person who proposes it. Misrepresentation and the deliberate misconstruing of another's argument are also common.

falling rhythm

A sound pattern in verse where the emphasis is thrown backwards onto the first syllables of the metric feet.

The dactyl and the trochee (*see* meter) have this effect. This example is from Shakespeare's 'The Passionate Pilgrim':

> Crabbed age and youth
> Cannot live together...

fantasy
A type of story (rarely set in verse) in which supernatural things happen.

These stories often include creatures from legend, myths and folk-tales such as dragons and unicorns. They are often set in a world of their own, an alternative existence. The protagonist is usually caught up in a large scale struggle between good and evil, and the outcome is almost always the triumph of good over evil. Some of the most popular fantasies are *The Lion, the Witch and the Wardrobe* by C. S. Lewis, *The Lord of the Rings* by J. R. R. Tolkien and *The Chronicles of Thomas Covenant* by Stephen Donaldson.

farce
A type of comedy designed to produce hearty laughter. It uses exaggerated characters in ludicrous situations, and techniques like slapstick and bawdy verbal humour.

fatalism
The philosophical notion that every future event is already decided and inevitable.

In literature this has been rendered as a pessimistic view of life, and the main characters in a novel or play or film that take this view are in for sad and depressing lives. Thomas Hardy shows a liking for this philosophy in his novels as seen in this extract from *Tess of the d'Urbervilles*:

> 'Did you say the stars were worlds, Tess?'
> 'Yes.'
> 'All like ours?'
> 'I don't know; but I think so. They sometimes seem to be like the apples on our stubbard-tree. Most of them splendid and sound—a few blighted.'
> 'Which do we live on—a spendid one or a blighted one?'
> 'A blighted one.'
> ''Tis very unlucky that we didn't pitch on a sound one, when there were so many more of 'em!'

Sometimes Hardy attributes the inevitability of the tragic circumstances of his characters to the manipulations of the gods (as seen in *Tess of the d'Urbervilles*):

> 'Justice' was done, and the President of the Immortals, in Aeschylean phrase, had ended his sport with Tess...

feature article
An expository text published in a magazine or newspaper that explores issues of current newsworthiness.

Feature articles are opinionative. Although they deal with facts and actual events they will be constructed to persuade the reader to a particular view of those facts and events. They can range from an editorial on an issue as serious as drug dependence to a light-hearted treatment of the Barbie doll phenomenon. They will usually use the layout conventions of newsprint (columns, photos with captions, large headline title and a by-line) to grab the reader's attention.

feature film
A fictional narrative film that usually runs somewhere between one and three hours.

The narrative can be complete fiction or a representation of true events. In either case, the film will be an interpretation of life, and will use techniques to persuade viewers to accept particular values and attitudes and reject others. For example: in *Dances with Wolves* (Kevin Costner) we are strongly positioned to see the Pawnee Indians as wild, warlike and ugly. There is no suggestion that these people might have been open to discussions about issues, or that they were exploited and betrayed by the white men.

The film contains traditional narrative elements such as character, setting, conflict and resolution. The narrative is shaped by the language of film which can be divided into technical, symbolic, audio and written codes which combine to create a diegetic effect or a compelling narrative in which audiences find themselves easily involved. Some of the elements of the technical code are camera angle and position, lighting, and juxta-position. Some of the symbolic elements are objects, setting, costume, body language and expression. Some of the audio codes are music, dialogue and sound effects. Some of the written elements are signs, sub-titles and credits.

Student example
The Full Monty opens with a replay of a 1960s documentary on Sheffield, England. The optimism and prosperity of those times are a stark contrast to the grim scenes of the 1990s that follow. The feature film, by opening in this manner, claims to be more than just a comedy. It is also making some poignant comments on the impact of urban recession on the lives of working class people.

Test your understanding
Write down a list of filmic techniques which you can recall seeing that signal a flashback in time. Which ones were most effective? Are there any that seem 'old fashioned'? What does that tell you about conventions of film?

feminist criticism

A school of literary criticism that challenges the patriarchal nature of texts and language.

Feminist critics argue that the traditional literary canon, the classic texts, reinforce the dominance of men in society and marginalise females. To overcome these problems they suggest:

- read texts against the grain—challenge the gender assumptions made by texts
- publish more texts by women and by writers who present alternative concepts of gender.

So you're hanging out in the ocean & the first wave of feminism has gone & the second wave & who knows how many other waves. It's dead flat & you find yourself thinking, Feminism - who needs it?
Aren't we post-feminist now?
Just be sure you can tell a fin de siecle from a fin de shark
horacek

See also fin de siècle.

Student example
Gwen Harwood's poem 'In the Park' presents a portrait of a modern woman who has devoted her life to raising her children. She is weighed down by them. The man who chances to meet her in the park is mobile and carefree. He thinks 'but for the grace of God ...', but does not finish this thought. Could it have been ... 'I might have been a woman, trapped and burdened, just like this one'?

fiction

Fiction is any text that tells a story without claiming to be historical truth.

Fictions which are based on facts are categorised as 'historical fiction' or 'fictional biography'. In recent years, the word fiction has become almost synonymous with novel, although the short story, the feature film and the stage play are also seen as fictions.

Defining fiction is problematic, since what makes one sentence 'true' and another one fictional? Most critics agree that a fictional sentence is one which refers to non-existent characters, places and events, and is not accepted as relating to the real world. The conventions shared by writer and reader of a work of fiction mean that the sentence is not open to the tests of truth or falsity applied to a sentence in non-fictional discourse.

The distinction between fiction and non-fiction is not always clear. A documentary film that claims historical truth may use fictional material such as detailed dramatic reconstructions.

Recent texts, such as the film *Wag the Dog* in which the President of the USA stages a war that everyone else thinks is real, have challenged our ideas of what we think is real or true. To what extent do any of our non-fiction texts pass the tests of truth or falsity?

See non-fiction.

figurative language
Language that exceeds the literal meanings of words to achieve a special meaning or effect.

Some of the most common 'figures of speech' are simile, metaphor and personification.

film—conventions of
The techniques and devices that viewers expect to encounter in a feature film or documentary.

Some of the most common conventions used are:
- the narrative time can be compressed and expanded beyond real time, but time will go forward with the progress of the film
- flashbacks in time will be signalled by either a camera technique (lose focus, etc.) or some other device so that we can recognise that these next events have occurred at an earlier time
- the camera will usually frame the character speaking or moving—some TV dramas like the ABC's 'Wildside' break this convention.

As with all conventions they are open to change and will be modified as the contexts in which they are produced change.
See conventions of film.

film language
The codes and conventions specific to film that allows film crews to make films, and audiences to interpret them.

See conventions of film.

film noir
A term originally applied to some American detective thriller films with low lighting and a sombre mood (dark film).

Now it is more widely applied to any film that takes a bleak outlook on life and portrays the darker side of human nature. Such films often contain endings that challenge the current orthodoxies such as having women getting away with murder or outwitting the men.

fin de siècle
The period leading up to the end of the nineteenth century. This term is associated with the French artistic movement described as Decadence.

Baudelaire, Verlaine and Rimbaud are some of the most notable poets of the period. Their work is characterised by a world-weariness and disenchantment with all that has come before. The poets praised artificiality above nature, the bizarre above the ordinary and the artist above the people of the middle class.

first person narrative
The voice of a character (who is involved in the action) telling a story.

See point of view, narrator.

flashback
A scene or event from an earlier time inserted into a narrative.

The term comes from the cinema but has been adopted into the language of print fiction.

focalisation
The specific focus adopted by the narrator of a story.

Many modern novels use a third person point of view that 'slides' from one character to another, revealing their perspective on the action. This can be called a change in the focalisation.

Student example
Sonya Hartnett's novel *Sleeping Dogs* uses a third person omniscient point of view with frequent changes in the focalisation to reveal the thoughts and feelings of many different characters. For example, the comment on page 26 'Oliver has buckled a child's mind...' is heard as Speck's perspective on the issue.

footnote
A note or additional comment added at the bottom (or foot) of a page.

foregrounding
Making one or more features of a text appear more important than others.

The techniques used to do this include such things as repetition, exaggeration and selection of detail.

form
The shape, style and structure of a text—as opposed to its content.

Often, the form of a text can be described by its genre—poetry can be divided into many different forms: sonnet, lyric, ballad, epic, pastoral, free verse, song, etc. However, the form of a text should not be thought of as a bottle into which the content can be poured to make a complete product. Form and content are inextricably linked although they may be discussed separately.

See categories.

formalism
A literary movement developed in Russia in the 1930s. The formalists tried to establish a scientific basis for the study of literature.

formal reports
A text explaining what has been discovered about an issue or idea set out in a strict way such as using scientific notation.

frame narrator
The storyteller who introduces and concludes a story.

This term implies that inside this frame some other narrator or narrators are presenting their stories; and the frame narrator is providing their telling with a context. Marlow's story is framed by the comments of the Company man listening to his story on board the *Nellie* in *Heart of Darkness*. Nelly Dean's story is framed by the various interruptions of Lockwood in *Wuthering Heights*.

Student example

In Anton Chekhov's story 'The Man in a Case' the main story is framed by the story of a teacher and a veterinarian. The teacher tells the vet a story of a Greek teacher who was so set in his ways that he gave up his chance of love. When the story is finished the listening vet wonders if he is like the Greek, leading an empty life constrained by rules. The framing narrative acts as a commentary, guide and a modifying influence on the story.

Test your understanding

If you have read a text with a frame narrator explain which of the narrators was set up as being the most reliable. What effect did the other narrator have on your interpretation?

See narrator.

free verse
A form of poetry that has no rhyme or regular rhythm.

It can establish rhythms and melodies of its own through the counterpoint of stresses and unstressed syllables. Some examples are many of the psalms from the Bible, *Preludes* by T. S. Eliot, 'Life-cycle' by Bruce Dawe and most of the poetry of e e cummings.

function
The place and purpose of a text in a culture.

To locate the functions of a text, examine ideas such as:

- what kind of audience does it appeal to?
- how does that audience respond to it?
- what ideas, values and attitudes does it encourage?
- how does it represent different groups in that society?

Test your understanding

Using a text you have read recently, answer these four questions as specifically as you can.

functional literacy
The ability to understand and control the codes and conventions of the English language, literature and culture.

This implies the ability to demonstrate such understanding and control through writing and speaking, and in listening, reading and viewing. Functional literacy is usually thought of as the ability to read, spell, and use grammar and punctuation correctly.

See critical literacy.

Gg

gaps

Gaps are places in a text where readers are expected to make the connections between one idea and another by using their knowledge and understanding of how their culture works.

Gaps should be distinguished from silences in a text. Silences are things which are not said by the text and which the reader is not invited to examine (*see* silences), usually because the text does not want to challenge certain cultural values. Newspaper headlines expect us to fill in a lot of gaps to make sense of them. For example, in order to understand this newspaper headline: 'Spider rubs himself out' (10 April 1999) we need to know that 'Spider' is a nickname for Peter Everitt, an Australian Rules footballer. We also need to know that 'rubs himself out' is a football phrase for 'makes himself unavailable for selection'. The headline also expects us to know that this refers to the recent case of Everitt racially vilifying an Aboriginal player in a game. We are also expected to fill gaps between ideas presented in the text. We understand that, in football, it is acceptable to physically assault another player (within the rules) but it is not acceptable to verbally abuse their ethnicity. We also fill in another gap—perhaps a more interesting one: Spider is empowered to impose his own penalty on himself. Is this because he is a senior player or because he is white, or because the players came to a 'gentlemen's agreement'? Some gaps we cannot fill and they will be left as questions.

gender

A cultural construct that defines the ideas of masculinity or femininity.

These ideas are based on the biological differences between males and females but go far beyond those genetic differences to create stereotypes of how men and women should look, behave, think and feel.

Different cultures construct different stereotypes for their men and women but in all cases anyone who looks, behaves, thinks or feels too far outside the defined limits will be marginalised or even cast out by that society. Texts usually reinforce this stereotyping by rewarding those who fit into the stereotypes and punishing those who do not.

Test your understanding
In the following stories, explain which gender stereotypes have been rewarded and which ones are strongly discouraged by being punished.

1 Cinderella
2 Star Wars
3 Rapunzel

generic conventions

The widely accepted techniques or devices that readers may expect to find in a text of a particular genre.

See conventions.

generic forms

The types of texts identified by the similarities between their conventions.

The major classical genres were epic, tragedy, lyric, comedy and satire. In modern times, the novel and the short story have been added as literary genres. Northrop Frye in his *Anatomy of Criticism* (1957) suggested that there are four major narrative genres (comedy, romance, tragedy and satire) that reflect the forms of the human imagination and correlate with the four seasons.

See genre.

genesis
The source or beginning of something.

The first book of the bible, Genesis, tells of how the world was made, how men and women were created and how, eventually, they were expelled from paradise.

genre
This term comes from the French and means 'type'. Texts are often categorised according to their features.

Videos in a video shop are grouped along the following lines: new releases, action, comedy, drama, children's, adult, horror, classics, etc. These categories are for consumer convenience as people who want to rent a movie for their six-year-old child do not want to have look through all the adult titles, and because those who want to see something funny do not want to search through titles including horror and war. Those people will have some clear idea of the sort of film they want to see, and if they can look in a section like children's or comedy they will probably be able to find a film that fits their expectations.

However, most texts belong in more than one category because they have features that fit several different genres; for example: Alfred Hitchcock's *Psycho* could be found in both the horror and the classics sections.

The same thinking can be applied to texts of any type.

Test your understanding
Using a text you have read recently, write down all the genres into which it could fit and explain what features of the text make this so.

gothic
In literature, gothic is a type of fiction that builds an atmosphere of gloom or terror, which relates strange or even macabre events and which often deals with disturbed psychological states.

Gothic texts include *Frankenstein*, *Wuthering Heights* and *Sleeping Dogs*. Examples of gothic musical groups are Alice Cooper and Marilyn Manson.

Greek tragedy
Originally a form of religious rite accompanied by songs in honour of the god Dionysus—god of fields, vineyards and wine.

From these rites, the Ancient Greek drama evolved so that by the fourth century BC Aristotle was able to define tragedy as:

> the imitation of an action that is serious and also, as having magnitude, complete in itself; in language with pleasurable accessories, each kind brought in separately in the parts of the work; in a dramatic, not narrative form; with incidents arousing pity and fear, wherewith to accomplish its catharsis of such emotions.

See tragedy.

Hh

haiku
A form of Japanese poetry that was originally governed by strict rules.

The rules are:

- the poem must be of three lines only and of seventeen syllables only, organised in a pattern of five syllables in the first line, seven in the second and five in the third
- the poem must express a single idea; it must move from a specific observation of a subject to an idea that provides the reader with an illumination—a new way of looking at that subject.

For example:

Bright bottlebrush stoops
tap-tapping on my window.
Oh yes! I am home.

There will usually be a 'season word' in the poem (a word that identifies one of the four seasons).

hamartia
The error of judgement that leads a tragic hero to commit a mistaken act.

It is sometimes referred to as the tragic flaw. The most common type of hamartia is hubris—or pride—that leads a great person to become arrogant and overconfident and thus to ignore their own reason or some important moral code.

See tragic hero.

hegemony
A group or number of groups coming together to wield power over others.

Feminist critics have used the term 'male hegemony' to describe the dominant group in societies in which women are disadvantaged.

hero/heroine
The central characters in a work of fiction.

The terms do not mean that these characters are particularly brave or noble. In fact, the heroine is often the helpless victim. Tess may be called the heroine of *Tess of the d'Urbervilles*—although the term protagonist is more popular now.

heroic couplet
Lines of poetry written in iambic pentameter that rhyme in pairs.

They are called 'heroic' because of their common usage in epic, heroic poems.

hierarchy
A ranking of people (or things) in grades or classes, one above the other.

Texts often set up social hierarchies without making clear the positions of some of the characters in that world. This is often the source of conflict in the story, as the characters try to locate their position or change it. Becky Sharp, in *Vanity Fair*, is a fine example of a character who does not accept her allotted position in the social hierarchy. That novel is the story of her attempt to change it.

Test your understanding
Write down a hierarchy that exists in your school or workplace—such as a list of awards in order of prestige. Then explain why each item is seen as better or more important than the next.

Homeric epithet
Compound adjectives that are repeatedly applied to stock nouns to create a strong link between the noun and those qualities.

The most famous are from Homer's *The Iliad*, for example: 'the wine-dark sea' and 'rosy-fingered dawn', and also 'swift-footed Achilles' and 'god-like Paris'.

homily

A sermon or written text intended to instruct and improve the audience morally.

hubris

The pride that causes a tragic hero to ignore the signs or the gods, or even their own common sense and commit some mistaken act that will lead to their fall.

See hamartia.

humanism

A philosophy that emphasises the basic goodness of humankind, believing that, through study and work, individuals can attain a kind of worldly perfection.

The humanists of the Renaissance period placed great emphasis on the study and imitation of the Ancient Greeks and Romans, especially on their art and literature.

Humanism finds itself in conflict then, with Christian belief which emphasises the sinfulness of humankind and concentrates on preparation for an eternal spiritual life.

Shakespeare in *Hamlet* (act 2, scene 2) expresses a view in sixteenth century England that would not have been possible in the fourteenth century or earlier:

> What a piece of work is man! How noble in reason! how infinite in faculties! in form and moving how express and admirable! in action how like an angel! in expression how like a god!...

Although at the end of that speech he adds: 'And yet, to me what is this quintessence of dust?' which is an idea that the fourteenth century Englishman would have understood immediately.

humour

The quality of a text that provokes laughter or amusement.

There are many different types of humour, some of which are pun, irony, satire, sarcasm, slapstick, parody and exaggeration/hyperbole. Why we laugh or smile when we see someone do something clumsy or silly may be explained by the fact that we know that we could easily have done the same thing ourselves, and we are very glad that we didn't. But not all humour can be explained in that way.

One theory says that when we tell a joke or story we set up patterns of words with which most of us are very familiar. We draw on the rules of narrative and, because we know what they are, we expect to hear certain predictable patterns of narration. When those expectations are shattered we are pleasantly surprised. The result can be that we laugh out of enjoyment and surprise. Those who may not be so familiar with that particular pattern of words will probably not get the joke.

> **Student example**
> In the satire and wit of the narrator of *Pride and Prejudice*, a humour is created that hides the dark and serious aspects of life so that readers can feel happy that everything has ended well for these women.

humours

In medieval times the body was thought to be made up of four fluids or humours: blood, phlegm, yellow bile and black bile.

The balance of fluids was thought to determine a person's disposition, character, mind, morality and temperament. Depending on which of the four humours was dominant a person's character could be:

- sanguine (hopeful, optimistic)—blood
- phlegmatic (patient, long-suffering)—phlegm
- choleric (irritable, angry)—yellow bile
- melancholy (sad, depressed)—black bile.

This theory had some influence on the works of Ben Jonson in *Every Man in His Humour* (1598), and the Elizabethan poets and dramatists.

hyperbole

A figure of speech that presents an overstatement or exaggeration for emphasis.

For example: 'She is as old as the hills!' or 'They haven't won a game for ages'. An example in literature occurs in *Macbeth* (act 5, scene 1):

> **Lady Macbeth:** Here's the smell of blood still.
> All the perfumes of Arabia will
> not sweeten this little hand...

hypothesis

A proposition or idea put forward as a starting point for investigation.

This must fit most of the known facts of the case and be capable of modification as the investigation develops. When readers read a text they set up hypotheses about what will happen next and what it all means. As their hypotheses either work out or are defeated, they modify them and create new ones until the text is finished.

See reading.

Ii

iambic pentameter

A line of poetry with five iambic feet. An iambic foot is two sounds or syllables; the first sound is unstressed, the second is stressed (given more weight or emphasis in its pronunciation). The word 'decide' is a good example of an iambic foot.

Iambic pentameter is the most commonly used metrical pattern in English poetry because it closely echoes the rhythms of natural (English) speech. The following (taken from Shakespeare's 'Sonnet 18') is a good example of a line of iambic pentameter: 'Shall I compare thee to a summer's day?'

icon

Something that acts as a sign for something else because it shares significant similarities. For example: a portrait is an icon for the person it depicts.

Germaine Greer, in her book *The Whole Woman*, sees the Barbie doll as an icon for the exploitation and subjugation of women.

ideology

A way of thinking about the world and people, including beliefs, values and attitudes.

An ideology works to advantage some groups of people above others. For example: manufacturers may share an ideology that includes beliefs like 'progress means making more things, more cheaply' and 'if people can buy better quality objects then they will lead happier lives'. These notions support the activities of manufacturers. Those people consuming the manufacturers' goods may also share those values—although some may not.

Ideologies are never neutral, obvious or natural—although most cultures will work to make their main ideologies appear so. The dominant ideology of twentieth century Western European culture has traditionally been that of white middle-class males since they have been the ones who have controlled education, the press and the governments. Examples of groups of people who have resisted the dominant ideology are Marxists and feminists—they have replaced the traditional beliefs and values with ones that advantage the workers and women respectively.

The significance of this term in the study of literature is firstly to recognise that this conflict between ideologies is often represented in literature and, even if the text tries to ignore or conceal its ideology, all texts have an ideological basis that will affect the way readers read the text.

idiom

Phrases that mean something other than the logical or grammatical meaning that one would normally expect from that combination of words. For example: 'neither here nor there', 'give us a break', 'no worries', etc.

idyll

Poetry that celebrates the rural life.

Idyll does not describe a form of poetry. Idylls are recognisable by their description of the simple country life as one of tranquil happiness.

See pastoral.

imagery

There are three separate kinds of imagery:

- the pictures conjured by a text in a reader's imagination
- the appeals made to our senses in a text—they are sight (visual imagery), hearing (auditory imagery), touch (tactile imagery), smell (olfactory imagery), taste (gustatory imagery) and sense of movement (kinaesthetic imagery)
- the figurative language used in a text, that is, the similes, metaphors, personification, etc.

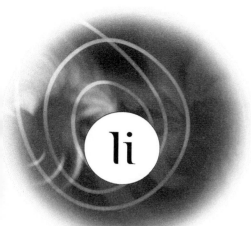

Student example

This extract is about *All My Dangerous Friends* by Sonya Hartnett.

The imagery in the scene before the climax prepares us for the violence. Images like 'the revelation ... bounded to the centre of the room' and 'The damage was bloody and jagged ...' emphasise the importance of Louie's betrayal and create an atmosphere of tension and danger. In fact the personification of the 'revelation' presages the exact action that Sasha will make in Daniel's house, and the surrounding metaphors of blood and violence foretell Daniel's doom.

imagination

The mental ability to receive images from the senses, reorder them, and transform them into new images and ideas.

imaginative writing

Writing that creates new order and new ideas out of material that is already known.

implied author

A literary created version of the real author, suggested by the tone and style of a text.

Test your understanding

Describe the implied author of this text.

We all agree that women should have equal pay for equal work, be equal before the law, do no more housework than men do, spend no more time looking after children than men do—or do we? If the future is men and women dwelling as images of each other, in a world unchanged, it is a nightmare.

(Germaine Greer, *The Whole Woman*)

implied meaning

A meaning constructed from the assumptions underlying the text or from the connotations of the words, one that is not present in the denotations of the words.

This is sometimes called 'reading between the lines'. We are told in *Heart of Darkness* that Marlow 'had the pose of a Buddha preaching in European clothes and without a lotus-flower': we imply that what this character tells us will be the truth.

Test your understanding

What is implied by these texts?

1 'We want women to be beautiful, to be capable, to be able to compete with men.' Wu Qing, Municipal People's Congress, Beijing.
2 'Let's just say the umpiring was something to see.' AFL coach, 1999.

indirect speech

Reported speech, as opposed to direct speech which indicates what a character has said by placing those words in inverted commas.

For example, 'Caitlin said, "Come in"' is direct speech. 'Caitlin asked him to come in', is indirect speech.

See direct speech.

inference

The process of drawing a conclusion from data or evidence.

This is an important part of the reading process where readers make judgements about characters and events from a limited amount of information.

intentional fallacy

The error of judging a literary work against the author's intention.

It is, of course, difficult to decide exactly what an author's intention might be, even if some readers consider it 'obvious'. In the case where an author has stated his intentions (as Henry James does in his prefaces to his novels), these texts can be taken into account in the evaluation of the text, but should not be given more weight than other elements of the author's context such as social context and ideological positions.

In a famous article, 'The Intentional Fallacy' (1946), W. K. Wimsatt and M. C. Beardsley wrote:

> One must ask how a critic expects to get an answer to the question about intention. How is he to find out what the poet tried to do? If the poet succeeded in doing it, then the poem itself shows what he was trying to do...

Postmodern critics point out that this argument is circular and underlines the futility of trying to discover 'intention'.

Student example
The inside track of the Beatles' *White Album*, when played backwards, asked, 'Will Paul be back as Superman?' Given the symbolism of the cover of their next album, *Abbey Road* where Paul was pictured as a body and the rest of the group were costumed as a priest, an undertaker and a grave-digger, it is clear that they intended careful observers to pick up the clues that Paul really was dead.

interior monologue

Writing that tries to reproduce the thoughts and feelings of a character just as they occur in the mind.

This may mean that the words, sentences and ideas are mixed up, not following the normal rules of grammar, syntax and logic as in this example from *Ulysses* by James Joyce:

> frseeeeeeeefronnnng train somewhere whistling the strength those engines have in them like big giants and the water rolling all over and out of them all sides like the end of Loves old sweet sonnnng the poor men that have to be out all night from their wives...

interpretations

Responses to texts, especially in relation to their meanings.

The following students have produced different interpretations of Robert Frost's poem 'Stopping by Woods on a Snowy Evening'.

Student example A
This short poem is a small pause in the life of the busy persona. He stops to watch a wood fill with snow just for the sake of it, even though he knows that others, even the horse, will think it is a 'mistake'. We appreciate the beauty of the moment, but he must hurry on because he has commitments elsewhere.

Student example B
Frost's persona takes a small pause in his journey and it acts as a memento mori—a reminder of his own mortality. There are the images of death associated with the woods: 'darkest evening', 'dark and deep'. The persona hurries to choose life, feeling that his life's journey is nowhere near completed.

Ian McEwan in his best-seller *Enduring Love,* provides an account of a story that receives two different interpretations. The story is about a dog that loves to sit in his master's favourite reading chair. One evening when the man came to sit in that chair he shooed the dog away. After a time the dog went to the door and whined to be let out. The man got up to open the door. Immediately, the dog darted back and leaped into the chair with a look of undisguised triumph on his face. McEwan writes:

> The writer concluded that the dog must have had a plan, a sense of the future which it attempted to shape...

This sounds convincing, but the second interpretation goes like this:

> ...ousted from its chair, it takes the next best place, by the fire, where it basks (rather than schemes) until it becomes aware of a need to urinate, goes to the door as it has been trained to do, suddenly notices that the prized position is vacant again, forgets for the moment the signal from its bladder and returns to take possession, the look of triumph being nothing more than the immediate expression of pleasure, or a projection in the mind of the observer.

As any sports fan knows there are always at least two interpretations of an umpiring decision that different groups of people will passionately defend—truly believing their interpretation to be the right one.

intertextuality

The interdependence of texts.

Any one text depends on all those that have come before it for both its writing and its reading. Texts share many things in common such as the language they were written in and the rules that govern that language. They also share the rules of the genre they were written in, as well as formal features—chapters, pages and titles.

If each text we read was all new to us we would be shocked and disoriented by every one. We would have to learn how to read each new text using a new set of rules!

These relationships between texts can be seen as forming a kind of woven fabric—an idea echoed in the derivation of the word 'text', from the Latin *textere* meaning to weave. The word intertextuality was coined by the literary theorist Julia Kristeva in 1966 to describe this 'woven fabric' of relationships between texts.

We could describe three main levels of intertextuality:

- At the level of language. All texts written in English share a common code. Even texts written in previous eras share most of these codes with texts written today.
- At the level of genre. The conventions that govern the way an individual text is written and read vary from genre to genre, but within a particular genre texts have a great deal in common. For example: most westerns include gunfights between heroes and villains set in the American West of the nineteenth century.
- At the level of allusion. Texts often make references to other texts, either by direct reference and quotation, or indirectly by paraphrase or imitation.

Student example

The feature film *Shakespeare in Love* is connected to many other texts, but most noticeably to the play *Romeo and Juliet*. They are both presented in English and share some interesting similarities of language structure and vocabulary, especially in the amount of Elizabethan English used. They both rely on narrative structure with characters who reflect each other in intriguing and sometimes comic fashion. For example, *Romeo and Juliet* is based upon a feud between two noble families; the film is based on the rivalry between two London playhouses.

The film also makes many direct references to the play when Shakespeare and his lover use quotes from the play to express their love for each other.

Test your understanding

Explain the types of intertextual connections you see in these texts.

1 I always thought it was a mistake, calling you Hamlet. I mean, what kind of a name is that for a young boy?...The nicknames! And those terrible jokes about pork.

I wanted to call you George.

(Margaret Atwood, 'Gertrude Talks Back' from *Good Bones*)

2 He turned up looking like Dracula, with a great black cloak and toothy grin. I told him, you'll not get a kiss from me tonight! And I reminded myself to put garlic on the shopping list tomorrow.

invocation

An appeal for help or inspiration.

This is usually addressed to a muse or god, but sometimes to a great poet/writer. Wordsworth invokes the spirit of John Milton at the opening of his poem 'London, 1802': 'Milton! thou shouldst be living at this hour...'

irony

The condition created by the difference between what is stated and what is actually the case.

In the simplest case, as in verbal irony, this is a tension that results when a statement's implied meaning is different from its literal meaning—or put even more simply: it is a case of saying the opposite of what you mean, for example: 'Oh, I'm sure you were the first to think of it!'

Situational irony occurs when there is a difference between what is reported and what we would expect in that situation. For example: Jonathan Swift's poem 'A Satirical Elegy on the Death of a Late Famous General, 1722' opens with this situational irony:

His Grace! impossible! what dead!
of old age too, and in his bed!

Another situational irony occurred in 1975 when Mr Michael Murphy tried to complete his record-breaking round the world solo cycle. He had cycled 25 000 miles, being robbed by bandits in Yugoslavia, stoned by tribesmen in the Khyber Pass and nearly froze to death in a blizzard. Through all this he was able to keep himself and his bicycle going. Not so when, only 40 miles from the finish line his bike was crushed in a conveyor belt at Heathrow airport.

issue/theme

An idea or set of ideas open to interpretation and debate.

Texts stimulate readers to think about particular issues. *Hamlet* may prompt thought and discussion on some or all of these issues: the nature of madness; the effects of patriarchal control on women; the needs of the family versus the needs of the State; and the consequences of revenge.

The issues that a reader sees as important in a text depend on their values and beliefs, and their reading practices. Because of the problems associated with the term 'theme' some readers/critics are now using the term 'issues' to open up debate on interpretations of the ideas presented by the texts.

Jj

Jacobean age

The period 1603–1625 in England covering the reign of King James I (in Latin, James is referred to as *Jacobus*).

This followed the reign of Queen Elizabeth I. It was a time of great literary activity, even the king published four of his own books (two of poetry, one of demonology and his *Counterblaste to Tobacco*).

jargon

(Old French—'warbling'—as of birds) Originally, unintelligible or secret language, now used disparagingly to describe the special vocabulary of particular trades or professions such as journalists, lawyers, sailors, computer specialists, etc.

journal

A record of events from a personal perspective.

This differs from a diary in that a journal is of a more public nature. Some famous journals include: *Boswell's Journal of a Tour to the Hebrides* and *The Personal Journals of Captain R. F. Scott.*

journalese

A derogatory term for writing that uses many clichés and formulae, and is couched in simple language, expecting an audience with a low level of literacy.

journey

A common element of narratives, often used as a structuring device.

Journeys, like stories, have a beginning, a middle and an end, and can be used to present the protagonist with a connected series of tests or challenges. Homer uses the voyage of Ulysses in this way in *The Odyssey*. James Joyce uses the same pattern in his *Ulysses*, but compacts the events into one day.

The physical journey can also be used to represent a spiritual or emotional one—so that a character grows and develops as they travel. Marlow's voyage in *Heart of Darkness* reveals a moral development that culminates in a moment of insight for him and the reader. Jack Kerouac's *On the Road* is a classic road novel that takes the reader on a joyful and illuminating journey.

See quest literature.

judgements

Making decisions and drawing conclusions about something.

In the case of making judgements about literary texts, this means that a text can be read and evaluated against a set of criteria or standards that a reader or a group of readers use to judge the suitability and value of the text. The key question about these judgements is whether or not the readers made them recognising the underlying values and beliefs they hold that allow them to come to their conclusions—and that not everyone will share the same values and beliefs. Therefore, not everyone will make the same judgements about the same text.

See ideology.

juxtapositioning

Setting one thing beside another, usually to act as a contrast.

Student example

In the opening of the poem ('Out, Out—' by Robert Frost) the beauty of the scenery is juxtaposed with the long and difficult hours of work that the young boy has to endure. This contrast highlights the lack of time he has for leisure or rest:

> And from there those that lifted eyes could count
> Five mountain ranges...

But the young boy is not one of those for he must attend to the buzz saw:

> And the saw snarled and rattled...

Kafkaesque

Writing in the style of Franz Kafka (1883–1924).

This term evokes the nightmarish atmosphere of Kafka's novels like *Metamorphosis* (1915) *The Trial* (1925) and *The Castle* (1926), and the short story 'In the Penal Colony'. These narratives present helpless individuals who are confronted by impersonal forces that provoke guilt, fear and the loss of individual identity.

See existential philosophy.

kinaesthetic image

A word or phrase that conveys a sense of movement; for example: 'scurrying', 'a flashing uppercut' or 'a swirling current'.

Künstlerroman

A novel that details the development of an artist from childhood to maturity; for example: ***A Portrait of the Artist as a Young Man*** **by James Joyce.**

Ll

language
Words and the rules and methods of combining them.

When you are asked to examine or analyse the language used in a text you are being asked to comment on:

- the style and choice of language used
- its effect on the reader's interpretation (*see* diction)
- the discourse that the text has used (*see* discourse).

To analyse the style of the language you need to consider three basic dimensions:

- Diction—or the choice of words. What type of words are used? Are they from common speech or a specialised discourse? Are they emotive? Or, attempting to be objective? *See* diction, style.
- Syntax—the order of words. This is particularly noticeable in poetry where 'normal' syntax is abandoned to produce rhymes and maintain rhythms. *See* poetic licence.
- Rhetorical devices—figurative language, rhetorical questions, invocations and exclamations. These techniques will usually have powerful effects on readers. *See* rhetorical device.

Test your understanding
Using these three dimensions, analyse the language of this text from Robert Browning's poem 'Fra Lippo Lippi':

I am poor brother Lippo, by your leave!
You need not clap your torches to my face.
Zooks, what's to blame? you think you see a monk!
What, 'tis past midnight, and you go the rounds,
And here you catch me at an alley's end
Where sportive ladies leave their doors ajar?

legend
A story about a supposed historical figure who achieves heroic status.

The hero often comes to represent some archetypal quality, for example: Robin Hood stands as a force of natural justice—redressing the imbalance of wealth by robbing the rich to give to the poor. King Arthur stands as a strong leader and civilising force. Joan of Arc stands as a self-sacrifice for the greater good. Cleopatra stands as a mysterious and powerful queen who refused to bow to superior force.

leitmotif
'A leading motif' (from German) that becomes important by repetition in a work or a series of texts.

Test your understanding
Darkness is a leitmotif in *Macbeth*. Find four references to darkness or shadow and explain how the accumulated images affect your response to the text. Or, choose another text that you have read recently and do the same thing.

limerick
A type of light verse that is composed of five lines.

Most limericks use five anapaestic lines, rhyming aabba and produce a humorous effect. For example:

There was a young lady named White
Who could travel much faster than light
She set out one day
In a relative way
And returned the previous night.

(Anon.)

limited narrator

A persona who tells a story from a position restricted to one main character.

This is still a third person point of view, so the narrator is not that one character, but they can relate the thoughts and feelings of that character. Usually, the narrator is confined to the limits of that character's knowledge and understanding.

See narrator.

linguistics

The study and analysis of language; of its elements and the principles of their combination and organisation.

In recent times, linguistics has had a significant impact on literary criticism since many theorists like Saussure and Chomsky have traced the ways that meanings are created in texts back to the effects and natures of individual words and phrases.

literal meanings

A meaning derived from the denotations of words.

This meaning will ignore the connotations or figurative meanings of words. It will not take into account 'implied meanings'. This phrase is often used as a criticism of someone's reading of a text, suggesting that they are being too narrow in the way they interpret the words.

See figurative language.

literati

Those who are in the know about literary matters. This term is not popular in recent times.

literature

There are two meanings of this term with important differences. The word can describe any text on a particular issue, for example: 'The literature on mineral exploration in the region'. It can also be applied to a much narrower band of texts belonging to the literary genres: epic, drama, lyric, novel or short story. In this sense, it often implies a judgement about the qualities of the work, but leaves unexamined who decides what those qualities should be, and whether a particular work has them.

Some readers have gone as far as to say that literature is any text that provides them with an aesthetic experience. Other critics have said that literature is any text that offers readers several choices in interpreting it.

litotes

A figure of speech that uses understatement for emphasis, and is therefore the opposite of hyperbole.

This is often used in normal speech, especially in Australia where people find it difficult to offer direct praise and couch it in litotes as 'What did I think of your performance? Yeah—not bad'.

lyric

Any poem that is not narrative and expresses thoughts and feelings through a single persona.

Sonnets, odes, elegies, dramatic monologues and most free verse belong to the lyric form. Lyric poetry is opposed to epic.

Mm

magic realism

A type of fiction that mingles the realistic with the bizarre and the fantastic.

These stories have complex plots, using myths, dreams and surreal elements. They use surprise, shock and horror to stir the reader. Most magic realist novels have been written by South Americans like Gabriel Garcia Marquez and Isabel Allende, although the Italian writer Italo Calvino and the English writers Angela Carter and John Fowles have experimented with this style. The South American writers, in particular, have used the form to make political statements. Marquez has said that, 'The writer's revolutionary duty is to write well'.

Test your understanding

Identify the elements of magic realism in this fragment of text taken from Gabriel Garcia Marquez's text 'A Very Old Man with Enormous Wings'.

...Pelayo and Elisenda very soon overcame their surprise and in the end found him familiar. Then they dared speak to him, and he answered in an incomprehensible dialect with a strong sailor's voice. That was how they skipped over the inconvenience of the wings and quite intelligently concluded that he was a lonely castaway from some foreign ship wrecked by the storm. And yet, they called in a neighbour woman who knew everything about life and death to see him, and all she needed was one look to show them their mistake.
'He's an angel,' she told them...

See realism.

malapropism

Using the wrong word; often producing a humorous effect.

The term comes from the character Mrs Malaprop, a character in Sheridan's play *The Rivals* (1775). Some examples from popular culture are: 'I'd like you to meet my daughter's fiasco' and 'That's a nice derangement of flowers'.

marginalise

To force something into the margins where it is either ignored or seen as unimportant.

This applies to the ideas and beliefs of particular groups whose interests do not coincide with the interests of the dominant group in a culture. Some marginalised groups have been women, some racial groups, homosexuals, the elderly, etc.

Texts may passively reflect the marginalisation of particular groups or they may draw attention to it, inviting the reader to challenge the thinking that has led to that group being ignored and marginalised.

Margaret Atwood has written many texts that give voice to marginalised groups. 'Unpopular Gals' from *Good Bones* is one:

> Everyone gets a turn, and now it's mine. Or so they used to tell us in kindergarten. It's not really true. Some get more turns than others, and I never had a turn, not one! I hardly know how to say *I* or *mine*; I've been *she*, *her*, *that one*, for so long.

Student example

Gwen Harwood's poetry examines some of the lives of individuals who have been marginalised in Australian society. In 'Suburban Sonnet' she presents us with a vignette of the life of a suburban housewife who has devoted her time to her children.

Marxist criticism

An approach to the reading of literature and culture that closely examines the nature of society presented by the text, especially in terms of the relationships that exist between workers and bosses (in fact, between the dominant and marginalised group), and the unequal distribution of power and wealth.

Many modern Marxist critics like Fredric Jameson are concerned with the political attitudes and assumptions in texts, especially those that remain unconscious or unstated by the text.

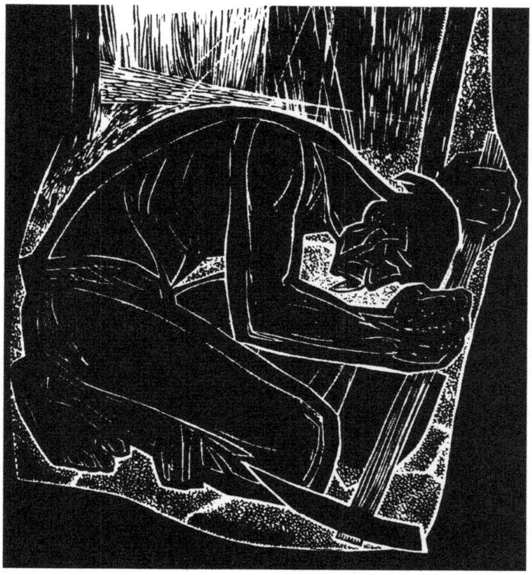

Student example

In Robert Frost's poem 'Out, Out—' a semi-rural family work scene is established. The boy is out in the yard sawing wood, his sister is in the kitchen preparing food, presumably others are nearby also at work. This scene of relative harmony is juxtaposed with the shocking speed with which the family turns from the boy after his death. The family situation at first seems harmonious but is distorted by the demands of working and surviving in a capitalist society.

matriarchy

A social group in which power resides with females and inheritance is passed down through the mother.

maxim

An idea, expressed in a compact way, that contains a general precept about human nature.

Maxims are closely related to epigrams and aphorisms. The French writer La Rochefoucauld (1613–1680) produced a book of maxims which are both entertaining and provocative. 'One gives nothing so freely as advice' and 'To refuse praise reveals a desire to be praised twice over' are two examples.

meaning

The connecting of one idea with another.

Readers make connections in the reading of a text, but meaning in a text is not a single thing nor is it something that the reader has to unwrap, like a present, as if the meaning exists somewhere inside the text. The meaning is created by the interaction of the text, the reader, the writer and their contexts. This diagram illustrates this idea.

Readers create meaning from texts in a particular context.

See interpretations.

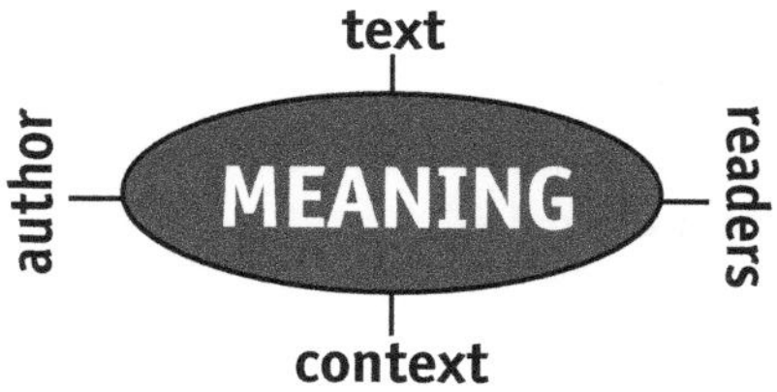

meaning systems/critical approaches

Ways of thinking about the world and the processes that particular groups use to make sense of their experience (which includes texts).

Some readers use a feminist perspective to explain their view of society and thus, when they read texts, their critical approach will be based on these feminist ideas. They will be particularly interested in the way the different genders are represented in the text, and how power is attained and used by each gender. Other readers will use different meaning systems such as Marxist, Freudian, postmodernist, etc.

medium

A means of carrying a message or idea.

Radio, TV and books are examples of the singular form of 'media'. Marshall McLuhan said, 'The medium is the message', emphasising the impact of the conventions and form of each medium on the meanings of the texts they carry. For example, our impression of a new music CD would differ somewhat depending on whether we heard about it in an advertisement on the radio or TV, or read about it in a magazine.

melodrama

Dramas that rely on improbable events and sensational action to evoke strong emotional responses in the audience.

The characters are usually flat types, being wholly good or thoroughly evil. The adjective 'melodramatic' is used as a criticism of the plot or action of a play or film.

memento mori

A reminder of human mortality.

This could be an object like a human skull that sits on a scholar's desk, or a literary motif that recurs in a text to reinforce ideas connected with death or old age.

Student example

In Robert Frost's poem 'Stopping by Woods on a Snowy Evening' the persona takes a small pause in his journey to watch the woods fill with snow. This pause acts as a memento mori, a reminder of his own mortality, since the images of cold and darkness connected with the woods fascinate him for a while, until he remembers the responsibilities he has to fulfil in life.

metaphor

A figure of speech in which one thing is described in terms of another.

This connection is implicit, whereas in a simile the comparison is made explicitly. For example, the simile: 'he ate his food like a hungry wolf' and the metaphor 'he wolfed down his food' are based on the same comparison but have different effects.

The metaphor often allows more than one characteristic to be transferred from the other object. Anthony Comstock described erotic literature with this striking metaphor:

> a moral vulture which steals upon our youth, silently striking its terrible talons into their vitals, and forcibly bearing them away on hideous wings to shame and death.

Student example

In Heaney's poem 'Digging' the persona connects himself with his ancestral fathers who have all been digging the Irish soil. The final metaphor implies that what he does with his writing connects him to these men.

> Between my finger and my thumb
> the squat pen rests
> I'll dig with it.

Test your understanding

Explain how the comparison works in these metaphors.

1 The courtroom exploded in anger.
2 He lurched into the bedroom and fell wrecked onto the bed.

Metaphysical poets

A group of seventeenth century poets who used a poetic style similar to John Donne's.

They were given a common name (even though they did not think of themselves as a group) by Dr Johnson in 1779 because he thought some of Donne's poetry presented arguments like the metaphysical philosophers. The main poets of this group were: Donne, Carew, George Herbert, Marvell and Vaughan.

meter (alternative: metre)

The pattern of stressed and unstressed syllables in verse.

The following meters are the most common in English verse:

iambic ∪ /
trochaic / ∪
anapaestic ∪ ∪ /
dactylic / ∪ ∪
spondaic / /

(where ∪ = unstressed syllable
/ = stressed syllable)

And the following terms indicate the number of metric feet per line of verse:

monometer—1
dimeter—2
trimeter—3
tetrameter—4
pentameter—5
hexameter—6
heptameter—7
octameter—8

metonymy

A figure of speech in which the name for one thing is substituted as the name of something with which it has been closely (and constantly) associated.

For example, 'The crown' for the offices of the monarch or 'Shakespeare' for his writings as in 'I've read all of Shakespeare'.

miracle plays

A type of play that dramatised the lives of saints, usually ending with a divine miracle.

They were popular in the Middle Ages, especially in France.

mixed metaphor

The combining of different metaphors.

If they clash this can result in some ludicrous descriptions.

> **Student example**
> The sun was a golden king
> settling in his throne
> and spread the skies with vivid marmalade.

However, this need not always be the effect. Shakespeare combines several metaphors in Hamlet's famous soliloquy in act 3, scene 1:

To be, or not to be, that is the question:
Whether 'tis nobler in the mind to suffer
The slings and arrows of outrageous fortune
Or to take arms against a sea of troubles...

See figurative language.

mock heroic

A style of writing that makes the trivial seem grand, and thus produces a satirical or comic effect.

modernism

A twentieth century movement in art, music, literature and architecture that deliberately broke away from traditional forms and ways of thinking about humankind's position and function in the universe.

In literature this meant that all the traditional forms and conventions were open to challenge and experiment. This resulted in works like James Joyce's *Ulysses* and the even more radical *Finnegan's Wake*, the poetry of T. S. Eliot and Ezra Pound, and the drama of Strindberg and Ibsen.

monologue

A speech by a single person. They may be alone or they may have an audience.

monosyllable

A word of one syllable; for example: 'pot' or 'trudge'.

montage

The placing of one (or more) camera shot next to another to create a particular response in the viewer.

When a director chooses to juxtapose shots they can be strongly related to each other, for example: a medium shot of a woman aiming a gun could be placed next to a close-up of the gun firing. We can make the connection ourselves. The Russian director Sergei Eisenstein thought that this was a limited way to use montage. His idea was to provide a collision of different images in which there was no strong linkage. A new understanding would emerge from the montage that was not inherent in any of the individual shots.

> **Student example**
> In the feature film *The Sweet Hereafter* (Atom Egoyan), shots of a man in a car in a car wash are juxtaposed with shots of a woman running to a phone box. This montage suggests a relationship between the two. Our guess is rewarded when she eventually phones him on his mobile and calls him 'Dad'.

moral
The lesson to be learned from a story or poem.

Aesop's fables often end with a moral, for example: 'Don't count your chickens before they are hatched' from the tale 'The Milkmaid and Her Pail'.

morality play
A dramatisation of the conflicts between good and evil in the human soul.

The main character, Everyman, encounters other symbolic characters such as Fellowship, Beauty, Good Deeds, etc. These plays were popular in Europe in the late Middle Ages.

motif
Any element that recurs frequently in literature. It can be an idea or theme.

The Carpe Diem motif is an idea that recurs in the poetry of the seventeenth century. It can also be a character such as the femme fatale of detective fiction or the fairy godmother from fairy tales.

muses
The nine Greek goddesses who preside over the nine arts.

They were all daughters of Zeus and Mnemosyne (Memory):

Calliope—epic poetry	Clio—history
Erato—love poetry	Euterpe—lyric poetry
Melpomene—tragedy	Polyhymnia—songs of praise
Terpsichore—dancing	Thalia—comedy
Urania—astronomy	

It was a common practice for a poet or writer to appeal for inspiration to the relevant muse at the start of the text. Homer begins his epic tale of Odysseus's return from the Trojan War in *The Odyssey* with this invocation of the muse Calliope:

> ...this is the tale I pray the divine Muse to unfold before us. Begin it, goddess, at whatever point you will.

mystery plays
A type of play based on the stories of the Bible.

The most common themes were the Creation, Fall and Redemption. In England these plays were often performed on wagons that could be moved from one place to another quickly so that an audience could see a complete 'cycle' of plays within a day or a few days.

myth/countermyth
A story that explains part of how a culture works and what it believes in.

Ancient Greek myths included gods and goddesses, and other supernatural figures. They explained such things as what happens when you die, why you should obey your parents or elders and how dangerous obsessions can be.

Since then we have added many of our own stories but our main myths are concerned with similar issues of importance in our society, for example: science, education and the family. Some of our myths about science are:

1 science produces progress and benefits for us all
2 science is objective and true.

There are so many stories that we share that demonstrate these ideas that there is not one that stands out—although Edison's painstaking work in the invention of the electric light bulb demonstrates the first myth. Charles Goodyear's luck in inventing vulcanised rubber when some sulphur spilled into a pot of rubber he was cooking on his kitchen stove might demonstrate a different myth about science!

There are countermyths to myths 1 and 2—often held by the same community that supports the myths. The countermyths to these two myths about science are:

1 science produces pollution and bombs that will eventually destroy us all
2 science is based on assumptions and beliefs that not all scientists agree on.

Some of the stories that demonstrate these ideas are *Frankenstein* by Mary Shelley and stories about the beginning of the universe.

See cultural myth, ideology.

mythology
A collection of myths or stories that explain why things are like they are and how a particular culture is going to operate, including its values, beliefs and practices.

Modern Western culture has its own mythology, just as the Ancient Greeks did, and the Romans, the Vikings and the Irish (to name a few cultures whose mythologies influence English literature and Western culture).

See myth/countermyth.

Nn

narrative (noun)

A story, usually presenting characters in a setting involved in some action or conflict.

narrative (adjective)

Describing the techniques and conventions by which stories are produced and read.

Stories present characters in a setting involved in a conflict. Many of the characters are recognisable 'types' such as 'the hen-pecked husband', 'the nerd' or 'the mysterious artist'. The writer selects their characters and the details of the story, organises these elements into a particular structure, and presents them through the voice of the narrator. This procedure of selection, organisation and presentation of characters in a story means that the values and attitudes of the writer will be bound up in the final product. The reader will experience these as an involving, engaging story often presented by an appealing narrator. This is one of the reasons why readers must become critically aware of the ways in which all texts are constructed. Even TV news programs and scientific reports use this process of selection, organisation and presentation, and therefore not only tell 'stories', but also present particular values and attitudes.

> **Student example**
> F. Scott Fitzgerald (in *The Great Gatsby*) has presented us with a few selected moments (as seen through the eyes of the narrator Nick Carraway) in Gatsby's story. This selection paints Gatsby in a flattering light and the omission of details about his shady activities with Mr Wolfshiem reinforces this perspective, so that we should approve of Gatsby's success, his generosity with money, and his ownership of Daisy.

narrative conventions

***See* conventions of narrative.**

narrative elements

Features of a text that are commonly used in stories.

Texts of any type can use narrative elements such as building up a description of a character or setting, explaining how one event occurred because of several others, or using flashbacks or suspense.

> **Student example**
> The documentary *Mabo: Life of an Island Man* uses narrative techniques to explain the achievements of Eddie Mabo and the grief that his family experienced after his death. It develops Mabo as a character living out his own story...

narrative position

The time, location and perspective from which the story is being related.

Some narrators tell the story piece by piece as the events develop, like Humbert Humbert in *Lolita*. Most narrators tell the events after they have occurred, so they have the knowledge of hindsight as they recount the story retrospectively. Some narrators tell their story from prison (so we know something of the ending already) and some from the deck of a boat about to undertake another voyage (as Marlow does in *Heart of Darkness*). These factors have some impact on the way we read and interpret the story. What has most impact are the values and attitudes of the narrator. To discover these things you need to ask questions like:

- how does this narrator represent men and women?
- how do they represent characters of different races, cultures, ages, etc.?
- how are we positioned as readers to think about the key issues in the text?

> **Student example**
> Pip relates his story in *Great Expectations* retrospectively, hoping to impress us with his naivety as a young boy and his strength of purpose as a youth. However, we see in his attitudes to Joe and the shock that he receives when he learns that his wealth and status has been bestowed by a convict, that he is just a poor little snob with only selfish and prudish values to offer.

narrator

The voice or consciousness that tells the story.

Authors have developed many different kinds of narrators to present their stories. First person narrators refer to themselves as 'I' and are characters involved in the story. Third person narrators are not involved in the story and refer to all the characters as 'he', 'she' or 'they'.

first person narrators

Storytellers who are one of the characters in the story they tell.

A self-conscious narrator will discuss the problems of writing or telling the story and make clear their involvement in the presentation (and interpretation) of the events. The narrator in J. D. Salinger's novel *Catcher in the Rye* begins his story like this:

> If you really want to hear about it, the first thing you'll probably want to know is where I was born, and what my lousy childhood was like, and how my parents were occupied and all before they had me, and all that David Copperfield kind of crap, but I don't feel like going into it.

A naive narrator, like a youth or someone not familiar with the culture that the story is about will report events without being aware of their meaning or significance. Gulliver in *Gulliver's Travels* (Jonathan Swift) narrates his stories of Laputa and the land of the Houyhnhnms in this way. As does Leo in *The Go-Between* (L. P. Hartley). The reader (who is not naive) is expected to fill in the gaps in the narrator's understanding, and does so by reading the contradictions and conflicts in the story.

An unreliable narrator presents an even greater challenge. Nelly Dean in *Wuthering Heights* conceals and exaggerates in her versions of Heathcliff and Cathy. The reader comes to understand her nature as a narrator and makes allowances for it. Other narrators are unreliable for different reasons. Meursault in Camus' *The Outsider* is detached and alienated from the world. The governess in Henry James's *The Turn of the Screw* is psychologically disturbed. We are still able to read these stories and construct our own version of events by doubting and questioning what the narrator says, and by giving more weight to what the other characters say, and by looking out for contradictions and clues in the text much like the way we do when we read a detective story.

third person narrators

An omniscient narrator is one who knows all, sees all, hears all.

They can report what is going on, for example, in London and Paris at the same time. They can expose the thoughts and feelings of any character; and they can look into the past or even the future as they see fit. Omniscient narrators can sometimes be intrusive. This is, they can interrupt the story to comment on characters or action, to pass judgement on them or challenge the reader to do so. Some of these narrators, like Henry Fielding's narrator in *Amelia*, can address the reader directly:

> ...my young readers...flatter not yourselves that fire will not scorch as well as warm, and the longer we stay within its reach the more we shall burn. The admiration of a beautiful woman, though the wife of our dearest friend, may at first be innocent...

Omniscient narrators can also be objective so that they only report what can be seen or heard. This gives the reader the impression that the narrator has disappeared—certainly their opinions and attitudes have not been made obvious—even though they will still be present in the text.

Alain Robbe-Grillet's novel *Jealousy* is an example of this:

> ...the boy, who appears at the corner of the house, carrying the tray with two bottles, three large glasses, and the ice bucket. The route he follows over the flagstones is apparently parallel to the wall and converges with the line of shadow when he reaches the low, round table where he carefully puts down the tray, near the novel with the shiny paper jacket.

A third person limited point of view confines the narrator to the experiences of one of the characters in the story. That character is still referred to as 'he' or 'she', but becomes the one readers associate with the most since we know more of that character's thoughts and feelings than any of the others.

Henry James's *The Ambassadors* tells the story of Strether's sojourn in Europe from a third person point of view, limited to the main character:

> Strether's first question, when he reached the hotel, was about his friend; yet on learning that Waymarsh was apparently not to arrive till evening he was not wholly disconcerted...

Test your understanding

Select any of the text fragments in this entry and explain the advantages and disadvantages of using that particular point of view in that story.

See narrative position.

naturalise

To make an idea or principle seem obvious and natural.

It is a self-preserving response of a culture to naturalise its own values and beliefs so that they are not open to constant challenge and disruption. Twentieth century Western cultures have naturalised the notion of a class structure in which the wealthy become richer and the poor become poorer. This condition is supported and made to appear 'obvious' by propositions like 'those who work hardest should get the most reward' and 'those whose work is of most value should get the biggest pay increases'. Such ideas can always be disrupted by a counter myth such as, 'those who can work should support those who cannot'.

naturalism

A kind of literature that showed a belief in nature; that everything could be explained by natural or material causes.

Much of this writing was dominated by the gloomy or seamy side of life—presenting characters struggling to live from day to day, unable to rise above their natural inheritance.

Louisa Ouida described naturalism as using realism in a restricted way, confining it:

> to what is commonplace, tedious and bald—(it) is the habit, in a word, of insisting that the potato is real but that the passion flower is not.

neo-classicism

A movement in literature and art that revived the value of the Ancient Greek and Roman authors; generally placed in the period around 1660–1780.

The main principles of the movement were harmony, proportion, balance, restraint and a thorough knowledge of the classical writers, especially Horace. There was also a strong belief in humanism. The main English writers of this movement were: Dryden, Pope, Swift, Fielding and Johnson.

new criticism

A movement in literary criticism that emphasises close reading of the text and argues that meaning is produced by the words in the text itself.

This school of critics was influential in the 1940s and 1950s, and developed as a reaction to the previous traditions of seeing a literary text as an expression of its author's thoughts, feelings and experiences. Some of the main proponents of this 'new criticism' are Cleanth Brooks, Robert Penn Warren and F. R. Leavis.

The main problem with this critical approach is that words and phrases do not have fixed meanings—so the meaning of a text must be dependent on the culture and context in which it is read; not fixed in the text for all time.

new historicism

An approach to literature that emphasises the value of researching the context of a text's production, consumption and status.

For example, the student who wrote the essay (excerpt on page 11, *see* author's context) in response to John Donne's poem has explored how some of the social conditions of Donne's time may have influenced the way the text was composed.

newspeak

A radical new version of the English language invented by George Orwell in his novel *Nineteen Eighty-Four*.

Its main purpose was to cut out the ambiguity of words and thus reduce the variety of thoughts available to people in the society of the novel; presumably to achieve a more stable society.

nom de plume

A pen-name.

Authors often use a new name to protect their privacy. Gwen Harwood made a habit of it—using half a dozen different pen-names (depending on the kind of poem she had produced) including: Walter Lehmann, Francis Geyer, Miriam Stone and T. F. Kline.

non-fiction

Texts that claim to represent historical truth.

Examples include biography, autobiography, travel literature, documentaries, journals and essays. The classification seems clear-cut but is not. Exactly what is truth or fact to one person may not be so for another. And no text can represent a fact and avoid the colour and influence of its writer.

> **Student example**
> The borders between fiction and non-fiction are not clear or fixed. Truman Burbank discovered this, along with the audiences, in the fiction feature film *The Truman Show*. He could not tell when the people around him were being real or putting on an act. We, the more knowledgeable viewers (who think we can tell illusion from reality), were asked to accept the TV producers as real!

See fiction.

non-print

A classification of texts that do not rely on the printed word as their main means of communication.

Examples include film, radio, TV and a drama production. Cartoons and advertising are made problematic since they rely on visual codes as well as written codes. Most commonly 'print advertising' covers all advertising in printed form, that is, images and/or words on paper. 'Non-print advertising' covers all other forms of advertising including the internet and word-of-mouth.

non-verbal language

Any way of communicating that does not rely on words as its main method.

Body language, tone, costume, music, facial expression and silence are examples. The codes governing the way these forms of communication operate can be complex and readers need to learn the details of how these codes work to be able to construct meanings with them. Texts such as film and drama use these codes extensively.

novel

An extended prose fiction.

The length of a novel allows for a more complex plot, more detailed setting and greater development of characters than in the shorter forms—the short story and the novella. The limits on the length of a novel are in dispute—although most novels fall into the range of 60 000 to 200 000 words. The novel in English is reckoned to begin in the early eighteenth century with works like Daniel Defoe's *Robinson Crusoe* (1719) and Samuel Richardson's *Pamela* (1740). In the late twentieth century many critics have proclaimed that the novel is dead—meaning that the conventions have changed so dramatically in the last hundred years that it is no longer the same form. However, despite (perhaps because of) the many experiments and changes the novel has been through it is still the most popular of the literary genres and attracts more prizes, more writers and more readers every year.

novella

(Italian—'little new thing')
A short novel that focuses on one situation or conflict and quickly produces a climax.

Examples are Conrad's *Heart of Darkness* and Steinbeck's *Of Mice and Men*.

obfuscation

A way of avoiding clarity in speech or writing thus clouding the issue.

For example: 'Students who do not avail themselves of the opportunity to request an extension to the deadline which has been set for the submission of this assessment will be required to produce written documentation by way of explanation in the event of a late submission'; and 'This does not mean that he refuses to believe that life is not worth living without a motor car'.

objective/subjective

Objectivity means being able to maintain a distance and detachment from the subject matter.

This suggests that a writer's (or reader's) feelings and prejudices will not affect the way an issue is presented in a text. This is problematic, since any writer's values and beliefs will be imbued in texts they construct. A text can only be 'objective' to the extent that the writer tries to avoid propaganda or makes their values and assumptions clear in the text itself.

Another meaning of this opposition is that an objective text is one in which the author appears to be absent, and does not refer to themselves or comment on the action or characters or issues. Texts like Browning's poems 'My Last Duchess' or 'Porphyria's Lover' are clear examples. A subjective text is one in which we are invited to think of the persona, the 'I', as the author. Wordsworth's poems 'Composed Upon Westminster Bridge' and 'London' are examples. Of course, critical readers will not accept this invitation, no matter how persuasive it may be.

objective correlative

A set of objects, a situation or a chain of events that a text sets up as being a trigger for a particular emotion.

For example, in *Macbeth* the washing of hands, especially in Lady Macbeth's sleepwalking scene (act 5, scene 1) acts as an objective correlative to the sense of guilt and despair felt by the characters and shared (to a greater or lesser extent) by the audience.

objectives

Targets set up for achievement—often stated in behavioural terms such as 'Objective 1: students will read three novels this term'.

ode

A long lyric poem of elevated style and lofty sentiments.

This was a popular form of poetry in the neo-classic and romantic eras of English literature. Writers like Dryden, Gray and Keats wrote odes in imitation of the styles of the Ancient Greek poet, Pindar and the Roman poet, Horace. Keats's odes are probably the best known: 'On a Grecian Urn', 'Ode To Autumn' and 'To a Nightingale'.

omniscient narrator

A storyteller who is in a position to know everything about all the characters and events in a story.

onomatopoeia

A figure of speech in which the sound of the word is an echo of its sense, for example: whoosh, splat, pop, bang.

In poetry, the technique is often used quite subtly. Ted Hughes in 'Bayonet Charge' wrote:

> ... hearing
> Bullets smacking the belly out of the air—

Coleridge uses it dramatically in his 'Rime of the Ancient Mariner':

> The ice was here, the ice was there,
> The ice was all around:
> It cracked and growled, and roared and howled,
> Like noises in a swound!

See onomatopoeia.

Student example

Karl Shapiro begins 'Auto Wreck': 'Its quick soft silver bell beating, beating...'. This line uses onomatopoeia to achieve two effects—the use of 'beating, beating' sets up the sound of a heartbeat and also helps create the dreamlike quality that pervades the first half of the poem.

oral tradition

The practice of singing or chanting or reciting poems from memory.

Poetry of the oral tradition precedes written poetry and is the earliest of all the literary forms. In some areas of the central Balkans it was still practised up to 1999 by bards who wandered from village to village reciting traditional folk tales and poems, and learning new ones to take to neighbouring villages.

oratory

The art of speaking eloquently and skilfully.

other

Those who are not 'us'. The strange ones.

This notion is used to expose the assumptions of texts based on oppositions of 'us' and 'them'. The 'other' could be 'all non-whites' in a racist text. It could be 'all non-Collingwood supporters' in a sporting discourse. By exposing and analysing the membership of both groups and challenging the grounds for making such judgements, these dichotomies can be deconstructed. In nineteenth century England this dichotomy looked like this:

Us	Other
white	coloured
Christian	heathen
civilised	savage
advanced	primitive

In a post-colonial society some of these notions still exist, but in general they have been replaced by an understanding of the value of a multidimensional, multicultural society.

oxymoron

A figure of speech in which two opposites are combined for a striking effect.

For example: 'A terrible beauty is born' from W. B. Yeats's 'Easter 1916'.

Student example

In act 1, scene 1, Romeo reacts to the scene of the brawl between the two houses:

...O brawling love, O loving hate...
O heavy lightness, serious vanity,
Misshapen chaos of well-seeming forms,
Feather of lead, bright smoke, cold fire, sick health...

These oxymorons encapsulate the conflict and its complexity. The clash of ideas like 'heaviness' and 'lightness' and 'seriousness' and 'vanity' not only represent the violence of the scene in words but also set up the difficulty these two families will have in trying to resolve their feud. The oxymoron might also be seen as symbolic of the meeting of Romeo with Juliet—two opposites coming together.

Pp

palindrome
(Greek—'running back again')
A word, phrase or sentence that reads the same backwards as forwards.

Examples include 'level', 'radar' and the famous 'Able was I ere I saw Elba' (which some claim was a lament by Napoleon—but he spoke no English). Also the possible first words ever spoken by man: 'Madam I'm Adam', to which the palindromic response would be 'Sir I'm Iris'.

parable
A short story with a moral whose main focus is to teach the listener/reader.

The parables of Jesus in the Bible are fine examples.

paradigm
The group from which items (or words) that are alike or connected in some way, can be chosen.

For example, in the sentence 'I love my dog' a possible paradigm for the word 'love' is 'adore', 'like', 'care for', etc.

paradox
A statement that is apparently self-contradictory but still holds an attractive truth.

Hamlet says: 'I must be cruel to be kind', a paradox often echoed in modern song lyrics. John Donne's poetry used many paradoxes such as in 'Death, be not proud':

> One short sleep past, we wake eternally
> And death shall be no more; Death, thou shalt die!

paragraph transitions
Sentences that link one paragraph of an essay (or any text) to another.

When a train of thought or an argument is continued from one paragraph to another there should be a connection between the last sentence of one paragraph to the first sentence of the next. This connection can be made by logic, theme, image, etc.

> **Student example**
> ...That episode of 'Foreign Correspondent' on ABC TV established my opposition to patriarchal systems and, a week later, reading *Sleeping Dogs* confirmed it.
> Hartnett's novel not only confirmed my views, but helped shape my understanding of how patriarchal systems operate...

paraphrase
Rewriting of a text in different words, but maintaining the sense.

There is some debate over whether paraphrase is acceptable as a critical response. Some critics will not allow it on the basis that the writer has already said it better and the paraphrase has added nothing to the original. Others suggest that all criticism is paraphrase.

parenthesis
A word or phrase inserted into an already complete sentence, to clarify an idea. This is usually done with brackets (although dashes can also be used).

parody

An imitation of another text in order to send it up or make it appear ridiculous.

This imitation can be in terms of subject matter, style, tone or even vocabulary. The imitation usually works by exaggerating a particular aspect of the original text, provoking amusement in readers. The success of the parody relies on readers having at least a vague knowledge of the original text. For example: this poem 'The Loving Song of R. J. Tangaya' by Sudesh Mishra expects that you are familiar with T. S. Eliot's poem 'The Love Song of J. Alfred Prufrock':

> Let us be going then, me and Baljit,
> When the evening is spreadeagling the sky
> Like Mrs Gandhi etherized by Sikhs;

pastiche

A cut and paste of different styles, texts or subjects.

Post-modernists use this as a favourite technique, especially in architecture. It has been said that this prevents people criticising post-modern work because there will always be some bit that will appeal to any taste.

pastoral

(Latin—'to do with shepherds') Any text that presents country life in a positive (often romantic) light.

It was originally song and poetry about the simple life of country folk in a peaceful and uncorrupted setting. Now it has evolved so that almost every art form has used the pastoral to present those nostalgic feelings of how we have lost the peace, love and perfection of a life lived in harmony with nature. An example can be read in Christopher Marlowe's 'The Passionate Shepherd to His Love':

> Come live with me and be my love,
> And we will all the pleasures prove...

pathetic fallacy

The technique of giving human feelings to nature, or allowing nature to reflect the feelings of a character or persona.

A fine example is the storm in *King Lear* which reflects the torment that the old king is going through, having been cast out by his daughters.

> **Student example**
> Finally (in *Four Weddings and a Funeral*) Charles and Carrie are reunited. They cling to each other as a rainstorm breaks and lightning flashes. The weather is almost a parody of their passionate meeting—pathetic fallacy at its best!

pathos

The feeling of pity and sorrow evoked by tragedy.

The death of Desdemona in *Othello* is an example.

patriarchy

A social structure in which wealth and power are handed down from father to son, and relationships are traced through the male line.

periodical

A journal or magazine published at a regular interval.

peripeteia

The turning point in a plot which signals a major change in the hero's fortunes.

In a tragedy, where the term is mainly used, this means a reversal of fortune, leading from prosperity to destruction.

See tragedy.

persona

The personality or mask adopted by a writer in a particular text.

The word derives from the Latin 'mask' used by actors in Greek and Roman theatre—where the actors took on a character to present to an audience. In some texts the persona is clearly different from the author, for example: Robert Browning is not the Duke of Ferrara in his poem 'My Last Duchess'. In other cases it is less obvious—but the narrating voice of *Vanity Fair* is not W. M. Thakeray—it is a persona. Nor are the voices of Gwen Harwood's poetry or of Virginia Woolf's novels the voices of their authors, even though they invite us to think so by speaking of themselves as writers.

Test your understanding
Describe the personae in the text fragments on page 66 (*see* narrator) by Salinger and Fielding. Then try the persona from the Browning poem on page 58 (*see* language).

See implied author.

personification

A figure of speech that gives human qualities to objects or ideas.

Time is personified as an old man with a scythe and a lantern. One version of this figure sits atop the pavilion at Lord's Cricket Ground, acting as a wind vane. The Statue of Liberty that stands in New York Harbour is the personification of an idea.

Alexander Pope personified the notion of:

Poetic Justice, with her lifted scale,
Where in nice balance, truth with good she
  weighs,
And solid pudding against empty praise.

See personification.

perspective

The position from which something is viewed.

In literature this includes the opinions, beliefs and values held by a reader or writer and how these affect the way they respond to a particular issue or event or character.

persuasive language

A way of writing or speaking that seeks to convince an audience of a particular idea or attitude by using a range of techniques.

Some of the techniques that are effective are the use of facts and statistics, humour, emotive terms, and appealing to the self-interest of the audience.

Petrarchan sonnet

A fourteen-line poem perfected by the Italian poet Petrarch (1304–74).

Usually the first eight lines form an octet and rhyme abba/abba. The second section of six lines (the sestet) rhymes cde/cde. It is traditional for the octet to set up a problem and the sestet to solve it.

phallocentric

Centred on the phallus.

Any social order where power is in the domain of men is called phallocentric. Feminist critics have used this term in their attempts to break down such oppositions as man/woman and masculine/feminine.

See representation (for a student example).

picaresque

A type of novel that tells the tale of a rogue and usually satirises the society in which they live, for example: Daniel Defoe's *Moll Flanders*.

plagiarism

Writing out someone else's work and claiming it as one's own.

This was a major problem for writers in Elizabethan times, but today copyright laws protect writers from plagiarism—although it does still occur.

Postmodern writers and critics find the idea of plagiarism a difficult one. Since, they say, a writer is a product of the culture in which they live and any text they write is a product of all the texts that have come before it, then a writer can do little more than reassemble what has already been written. At what point, they ask, does reassembly become plagiarism? Shakespeare, for instance, would probably have read or heard the lines from Munday's plays (1598):

> The multitudes of seas dyed red with blood;

and

> And made the green sea red with Pagan blood.

Shakespeare has reassembled these lines in *Macbeth* (act 5, scene 2):

> the multitudinous seas incarnadine,
> Making the green one red.

plot

The design or structure of events in a story to produce curiosity and suspense in readers.

There are three plot questions readers ask:

- why did that happen?
- why is this happening?
- what will happen next and why?

It is important to distinguish plot from story because plot conveys the idea of the constructedness of the text—the events and the reasons for them have been organised to provoke those three questions.

The novelist E. M. Forster did this best in *Aspects of the Novel* (1927):

> 'The king died and the queen died' is a story. 'The king died, and then the queen died of grief' is a plot.
>
> The time sequence is preserved, but the sense of causality overshadows it. Or again: 'The queen died, no-one knew why, until it was discovered that it was through grief at the death of the king'. This is a plot with mystery in it, a form capable of high development.

A plot can be seen as a story with its events reordered. Plots are usually organised into an exposition, a complication, a climax and a resolution. Some texts have episodic plots—each chapter presents a new episode or incident in the life of a main character, as in *The Adventures of Huckleberry Finn* by Mark Twain. Other texts disrupt expectations about traditional plot structures by offering two different endings, as in *The French Lieutenant's Woman* by John Fowles. B. S. Johnson presented his novel *The Unfortunates* in a box. The first and last chapters were clearly labelled but the readers were invited to shuffle the others around in any order they pleased!

See structure.

poetic conventions

***See* conventions of poetry.**

poetic diction

The vocabulary used in poetry.

This was a fashionable idea in the eighteenth century when poets used a particular kind of language and people in everyday life used a different kind. Thomas Gray, the poet, observed that language must be selected according to the work in hand. In the nineteenth and twentieth centuries the argument has been reversed and poetry must now use the common language of the people if it is to communicate.

See language.

poetic justice

The handing out of a character's (or characters') just reward at the end of a play or story.

The evil are punished and the good rewarded. This notion was going out of fashion by the end of the seventeenth century but is maintained today in genres like detective fiction and family dramas.

poetic licence

The freedom given to a poet to change words or phrases to suit the poem.

For example:

> **At Leeds**
>
> Here lies my wife,
> Here lies she;
> Hallelujah!
> Hallelujee!

The ecstatic anonymous poet has invented the last word using poetic licence.

poetry
Traditionally defined as a metrical composition.

In recent times, a lot of verse has been written that has no regular rhythm, particularly prose-poetry and some free verse. The term 'poetry' has long been used to oppose the term 'verse', to indicate a superior type of composition.

Poetry has often been divided into two types: narrative and lyric. The narrative forms are epic, ballad and dramatic monologues. The main lyric forms are sonnet, ode, elegy, free verse and song.

Some of the more famous attempts to define poetry are:

> Poetry is the breath and finer spirit of all knowledge: the impassioned expression which is in the countenance of all science; the spontaneous overflow of powerful feelings. It takes its origin from emotion recollected in tranquillity.
>
> (William Wordsworth)

> Poetry is the best words in the best order.
>
> (Coleridge)

> Poetry is the pains of turning blood into ink.
>
> (T. S. Eliot)

> Poetry is a counterfeit of the communication of those who communicate by silence.
>
> (Randolph Stow)

> A poem, very briefly, is a short novel you can fox-trot to.
>
> (Fred Dagg)

point of view
The perspective from which a narrator presents a narrative.

If we imagine a story being delivered orally then there are three possible positions for the storyteller to adopt in relation to the characters in the story and the people listening:

- first person—the narrator is a character in the story and refers to himself or herself as 'I'; the other characters are 'he', 'she', etc.
- second person—the narrator directly addresses the listening audience and refers to them as 'you'; the narrator uses this word to include the audience as a character in the story (this is rarely done)
- third person—the narrator tells a story that neither they nor the audience are involved in; all the characters are referred to as 'he', 'she', etc.

Student example

In *That Eye, the Sky*, Tim Winton uses the young boy, Morton Flack, to narrate the story of his family. This first person narrator is naive, but full of energy and love for all the characters around him. By using such a narrator, Winton is able to explore sensitive family issues with compassion and present complex spiritual themes that readers of all ages can engage with.

See narrator.

polysemy
The way in which words or texts are capable of meaning more than one thing.

A polysemic reading of a text would emphasise the fact that readers are capable of interpreting words, sentences and whole texts in several ways. *See* interpretations.

What's your interpretation? Can you explain why?

portmanteau word

A word formed by combining two or more words.

A portmanteau is a large bag—a carry-all. A portmanteau word is designed to carry two or more meanings. Lewis Carroll is well known for his playfulness in creating many portmanteau and nonsense words, especially in poems like 'Jabberwocky'. For example, 'whiffling' could be a combination of 'whistling' and 'shuffling', something a Jabberwocky is likely to do!

post-colonialism

A reaction to the values and attitudes of the colonial era in which white European culture was forced upon the less fortunate peoples of the world because it was seen as more civilised and more progressive.

Post-colonial literature includes writing by those peoples of the colonised nations, providing a voice responding to the actions and culture of the Europeans. Most notable are the poetry of the Caribbean, the novels of South Africa and India, and the emerging art of the Aborigines in Australia. A post-colonial critical perspective can be adopted by readers who are interested in the effects of one culture on another, foregrounding issues such as cultural identity and race.

post-modernism

A reaction against modernism and the horrors of the Second World War.

In literature this has meant a rejection of the forms and conventions developed in the first half of the twentieth century (which were themselves a reaction against previous traditional forms and conventions). Some examples of postmodern experiments are Theatre of the Absurd, magic realism and pastiche in novels, and concrete poetry. The main distinguishing feature of the movement is the feeling that life is meaningless and often cruel, and that those things that were previously thought to be solid and certain are now revealed to be ambiguous and changeable. Even language is shown to be so unstable that any meaning we create is seen as a temporary illusion.

John Fowles in *The French Lieutenant's Woman* openly discusses the problems he has in ending his story and wants to give up his role as a constrictor of the story:

> Fiction usually pretends to conform to the reality: the writer puts the conflicting wants in the ring and then describes the fight—but in fact fixes the fight, letting that want he himself favours win...
>
> But the chief argument for fight fixing is to show one's readers what one thinks of the world around one—whether one is a pessimist, an optimist, what you will. I have pretended to slip back into 1867; but of course that year is reality a century past. It is futile to show an optimism or pessimism, or anything else about it, because we know what has happened since...

And there are levels of uncertainty as F. Parke demonstrates humorously in the novel *Greenfire*:

> I've pieced all this together from letters, journals, notes on scraps of paper, official documents and newspapers and most of all from my memory. As you know I've had to change the names for fear that people don't like to hear of the misdemeanours or faint hearts of their ancestors. But you can be sure that most of what I tell you is true—more or less—and that anything someone disputes is just a failure of my memory—or someone else's.

Terry Eagleton summarised post-modernism's refusal to look for grand-narratives or deeper meanings in things as follows:

> post-modernism... has outlived that (desire) to scratch surfaces for concealed depths; it embraces instead (a view)... for which the world—would you believe it?—is just the way it is and not some other way.
>
> (1985)

post-structuralism

A reaction against structuralism, emphasising the possibility of many different readings of a text.

The main proponents of post-structuralism are Jacques Derrida, Roland Barthes and Julia Kristeva (the French have been the main contributors to theories about language and literature in the second half of the twentieth century). The most common reading practice of these critics is deconstruction.

See structuralism, post-modernism.

power

The ability of one person to influence another.

The way power is distributed in a society (real or fictional) is an important factor for many readers. Feminist and Marxist readers in particular want to question the way power is attained and used in texts—especially when it is used to silence or marginalise one group and promote the interests of another.

praxis

The current practice or accepted ways of doing things.

précis

A summary of a long work.

predictions

Informed guesses about what might happen in the future.

This is an important part of the reading process. Readers will make inferences and predictions about characters and events based on what they know about texts like the one they are reading, information provided by the text, and information already provided by the context. When readers make accurate predictions they are reassured that their reading of the text is well founded. When they make predictions that do not come true, they are surprised by what does happen and modify their original predictions to take account of the new developments. Clearly, a text that keeps its readers reading must find a balance between the two effects.

Student example

In H. E. Bates's story 'The Good Corn' I expect that Mrs Mortimer will find out that her husband, Joe, is the father of Elsie's child and confront him with the facts. However, the story leads me to think that she will not be able to force him to leave home, nor will she have the power to go away on her own. This is because all the personal and economic power belongs to Joe...

See reading.

preface

An introduction to a long work in which the author often gives the reader hints or guidelines on how to read the main text.

preferred reading

***See* dominant readings.**

prelude

An introduction to a work that foreshadows its main themes.

premise
A starting point or idea.

Logical arguments begin with some premises and move to conclusions.

privileging
To give advantages to some group or idea, over others.

Texts can be said to privilege a particular view of the world and ignore others. The opposite of 'privilege', in this sense, is 'marginalise'.

> **Student example**
> Robert Frost's poem 'Never again would birds' song be the same' privileges Adam's (men's) position in the world and turns Eve's role into something close to that of the animals. She is natural, sweet, decorative—and powerless.

See marginalise.

prologue
The opening section of a literary work—often found in a play or long poem.

The prologue to *Romeo and Juliet* is well known:

Chorus: Two households, both alike in dignity,
In fair Verona, where we lay our scene,
From ancient grudge break to new mutiny,

proofread
To read through a text and mark errors for correction—especially errors in the surface features (punctuation, spelling, grammar and paragraphing).

See surface features.

propaganda
Texts devoted to the purpose of spreading a particular idea or belief.

When a text steps over the line between arguing a particular philosophical or ethical case and becoming propaganda is open to debate. A lot of literature can be didactic, teaching or instructing its audience, yet avoid the label of propaganda. Harriet Beecher Stowe's novel *Uncle Tom's Cabin* puts up a strong case against slavery in the Southern states of America. Readers would have to decide for themselves whether it is propagandist literature or not, depending on their interpretation of the purposes of the text.

proposition
An idea put forward for discussion or argument.

Some essay models require a proposition to be presented in the first paragraph so that the reader clearly understands what is being argued in the rest of the essay.

> **Student example**
> (The proposition is highlighted in italics.)
>
> The play *Macbeth* by William Shakespeare is one of the best known portrayals of witches. It dramatises the story of a Scottish noble who is influenced by three witches to murder his king and seize the crown for himself. The conflicts this embroils him in are represented by various opposing elements, the most notable being the conflict between the supernatural and natural worlds. *It is this opposition that most powerfully influences our interpretation of the play.*

See essay.

prose
An ordinary, unadorned style of writing or speaking.

Prose is opposed to poetry in that it has no regular meter or rhythm. Shakespeare's workers often speak in prose while the nobles get all the poetry, although, as some readers have pointed out, witches and madmen are not just restricted to prose.

protagonist
The main character or hero in a story.

The word comes from the Greek meaning 'first combatant' and was used in Ancient Greek tragedy to describe the principal actor. The deuteragonist and the tritagonist were the second and third actors. In most plays and stories the protagonist will be opposed by an antagonist.

See antagonist.

Student example

William Blake's poem 'The Sick Rose' is a short poetic warning to young women to beware the sexual advances of young boys. The rose represents perfection and is the flower of the Roman goddess of love. It is usually seen as a symbol for the female genitals and the worm that destroys it represents the male phallus. The poem works strongly at the subconscious level...

proverb
A short, concise saying that sums up a general truth or belief.

Post-modern readers enjoy the Ancient Greek proverb: 'We cannot step twice into the same river'. Post-structuralists have varied that to: 'We can't step into the same river once'.

pseudonym
(Greek—'false name')
A name adopted by a writer, possibly to protect their privacy. Also called 'nom de plume'.

psychoanalytic criticism
A way of reading texts that emphasises the unconscious dimensions of subjects and language.

This reading practice is based on the works of Sigmund Freud and developed by the work of Jacques Lacan. It often interprets elements of the text at the symbolic level, for example: snakes or worms may represent male genitals or power, shells or roses may represent female genitals or receptiveness.

purple patch
A piece of writing that stands out from its surrounding text as being particularly grand or poetic.

This is usually seen as a fault, or a lapse in style, but it can be used successfully. Shakespeare uses it in several plays to draw attention to the style and content of a speech—as with John of Gaunt's dying speech in *Richard II* (act 2, scene 1, lines 40ff):

This royal Throne of kings, this scept'red isle,
This earth of majesty, this seat of Mars,
This other Eden, demi-paradise
This fortress built by Nature for herself
Against infection and the hand of war,
This happy breed of men, this little world,
This precious stone set in the silver sea...

purpose
What the text is trying to achieve.

If you ask what is the author's purpose you may end up with answers like 'to get rich', 'to become famous', etc. which may be true but are not very revealing. If you ask, 'What is the text's purpose?' you may be more fruitfully involved in an examination of the ideas, values and attitudes that the text is presenting.

quatrain

A stanza of four lines. These lines can be rhymed or unrhymed; they may have a regular meter.

quest literature

Texts that use a journey as a major structuring device.

The journey or voyage is usually a search for something valuable or to overcome a wrong that has been done. The stories of the Quest for the Holy Grail, set in Medieval England, are classic examples. King Arthur's knights search for the cup used by Christ at the last supper, knowing that only the worthiest knight will find it.

Frodo in Tolkien's *The Lord of the Rings* journeys into the heart of evil (Mordor) to destroy the ring that would give Sauron the power to rule the worlds. Such quests are often undertaken by the unlikeliest characters who must overcome obstacles in their own make-up as well as those presented by the physical manifestations of evil. Traditional quest stories end in success when the hero finds their heroic nature, overcomes evil and returns to the 'normal' world.

The journey or quest can often be interpreted as an allegory for a journey through life or the emotional and spiritual development of a character.

quotation

Writing out a fragment of some other author's text for the purpose of clarifying an idea or to draw attention to some aspect of that fragment.

In essays or discussions about particular texts you will probably be required to quote from those texts to support your ideas or interpretations. This is done by placing the exact words used in the text into inverted commas (or differentiating the text from the body text in some way, for example: indenting the quote or using a smaller font size), giving the page number or source of the quote, and then explaining how this fragment of text supports the points you are making. There are several referencing systems, for example: the Harvard system, the Vancouver system, amongst others.

The Harvard system is now widely adopted, although different schools and universities hold individual preferences. Always find out what system of referencing and quoting your school favours.

Rr

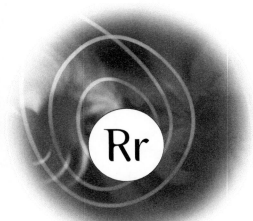

race/ethnicity

An idea invented to distinguish between groups of people on certain arbitrary characteristics such as skin colour or nose size.

The idea of belonging to a group on the basis of inherited physical traits is a socially constructed notion, and it is taught in schools and learned through the media and literary texts. The idea has been a popular one because it has provided groups in power with justifications for excluding other groups from power.

This idea is important in the study of literature because literary texts either reinforce or challenge the cultural construction of 'race' or 'ethnicity'. Some texts may ignore the idea and thus make the marginalised racial group disappear altogether!

In reading texts we need to ask what stereotypes or representations of race are being offered, what values and attitudes towards those groups we are being invited to accept, and whose interests are being served by such positions.

> **Student example**
>
> In his play *No Sugar*, Jack Davis presents the interactions between the dominant white culture and Aborigines. By representing the Aborigines as victims of race stereotyping and as the 'preferable other', Davis challenges the dominant constructions of Aboriginality and asks white Australians to reassess their attitudes.

rationalism

The idea that rational order can be found in the universe and that the power of reason can understand it.

The eighteenth century is often referred to as the era of rationalism. René Descartes (1596–1650) was one of the first 'rationalists' trying, in his philosophical method, to show that the power of reason is all we need to understand ourselves and the universe. His famous statement, 'I think, therefore I am' was the starting point for his philosophy.

reader positioning

The way texts invite readers to accept certain ideas and adopt particular attitudes towards a subject or issue.

This is done by employing certain techniques such as using statistics or experts; emotive or persuasive language; a particular point of view; attractive, sympathetic characters to illustrate or explain views and enact values; and many other techniques, depending on the genre of the text. It is important to recognise that few authors are trying to 'manipulate' readers by fooling or tricking them—these techniques are part of the accepted conventions of texts and not weapons in a war against readers. Most writers will try to position their readers to see their point of view on an issue, but readers will probably already have some opinions and ideas on the subject and those will not be transformed overnight.

As a reader you start reading a text with a set of values and attitudes about the subject matter of the text. It might be a book about teenagers and drugs. Whether you're a parent, a dealer or a teenager yourself, you'll already hold views and opinions on the issues to be discussed. Your views may be: the sale of all drugs should be made illegal to anyone under twenty-one; teenagers need as much information about drugs as they can get; or teenagers should be allowed to experiment with any drug.

The writer of the book will also have some views on the issues. They will try to convince you and other readers that their views are the right ones. Probably they will try to persuade you that you should change your attitudes and ideas. To do this they will use a range of techniques such as statistics, experts and their opinions, emotive language, etc. This is called positioning the reader.

See rationalism.

Readers, of course, can reject this attempt to change their views and attitudes, although while they are reading the text there is a strong invitation to participate in the thinking that leads to those values and attitudes.

Some of the most powerful techniques to position readers are: using attractive, sympathetic characters to illustrate and expound the views and attitudes; using 'facts', statistics and logic to convince readers; and using strong emotive language and details to stir or shock the reader.

Student example

Thea Astley's *It's Raining in Mango* presents us with a compelling picture of the Australian Aborigines as a 'dispossessed people' who have been marginalised and victimised by the dominant white culture. As readers we are positioned by her sympathetic voice to view them with the same compassion.

Test your understanding

Explain how you are positioned in relation to McDonalds by the four different texts on pages 84 and 85 (*see* reading).

reader response

The theory that argues that a reader makes a significant contribution to the meanings of a text.

The context in which the text is read and the reader's education and cultural background are some of the important factors that influence the way the reader responds to the text.

reader's context

The great number of factors that shape the way a reader interprets a text.

These factors are a product of competing beliefs and cultural practices and knowledge in the reader's culture. Some of the factors that may influence an individual reader's context are their background and education, ideology, gender, religion, age, etc.

A reader's context is always changing—which is one of the reasons a reader might read a novel twice and come up with two quite different responses.

Test your understanding
Write down the main factors that contribute to your context as a reader of the daily newspaper, or some other text that you have read recently. Be as specific as you can.

reading

The process by which an individual and a group of people make meaning from text.

This will be influenced by the text itself, the rules and practices of the culture, the beliefs and values of the individual and the culture, the reader's previous experience with similar texts, and other like factors of the reader's context.

People have been taught to be good readers and usually produce readings of texts that agree with one another so closely that their interpretation appears to be 'obvious' or 'natural'. This is called the 'dominant reading'. Any other reading, may, at first glance, seem to be perverse. This is because our reading of a text uses a commonly agreed upon set of rules and applies a widely held set of values and beliefs to fill in the gaps in the text and make sense of the whole thing.

Not every reader will produce the same reading. They may not accept the rules that the culture in which they are reading the text has agreed. An example of this might be the way two different readers react to the phrase, 'They were dressed in mourning'. Some readers will imagine people dressed in black. Some Chinese readers will imagine people dressed in white.

Some readers may not share the same values and beliefs as those who have produced the 'natural' reading, for example: to many readers the phrase, 'at the time of Australia's first settlement' means about 200 years ago. To many others it means about 40 000 years ago. Many readers will read 'The minister promised a package of workplace reform' as hope for improved business practices. Many others will see it as a threat to their present working conditions and still others will read it as another empty promise attempting to win votes. The last two are resistant readings—although you might argue that so many people have lost their trust in politicians nowadays that the last reading has some claim to be the dominant one.

Some readers will not share the same experience of texts as others. An example of this is how two different readers might read the nursery rhyme 'A Ring-around-a-Rosie'. A young child may read it as an invitation to dance in a circle and then fall down. Someone who is used to researching the origins of such texts may add to that reading and see it as a frightening statement about the effects of bubonic plague. This is an alternative reading.

Test your understanding
Read the four student responses to a recent TV advertisement.

What are the main factors in each reader's context that have produced these readings? Cultural background? Values and beliefs? Past experience? Or, something else?

See resistant readings/reading against the grain.

Student A
This is a really cool ad. Maccas really know how to appeal to kids our age by using 'The Simpsons' to promote their food. I like the music too. And the burgers look pretty appetising.

Student B
This ad reminds me of how unhealthy this kind of food is. The burgers are presented as being good to eat, and the fries look clean and crisp but I know that all fast food chains work on two principles—use lots of salt to enhance any flavour the food might have and use lots of fat so that it slides down easily. Yuk!

Student C
I know the girl in this ad—Peta. She works at Maccas in the city. She was a good choice for the ad as she's pretty good looking and always smiling. She's the kind of person that makes you think you should run in to get a burger just to be served by her.

Student D
I hate looking at this ad as I've read that companies like this one are responsible for cutting down hectares of forest every day just to supply the packaging for their products.

realism
An attempt to represent the real world in text.

This is a problematic idea since what is 'real' or 'realistic' to one person may well seem quite 'unreal' to another. For example: the visits of Pip to Miss Haversham's place in *Great Expectations* may be read as fantastical and symbolic or as a realistic account.

The literary movement of the nineteenth century that was called 'realism' set out to oppose romantic fiction and present an accurate imitation of life. The novels of Flaubert and Balzac are examples of this movement. This idea was pushed to its extreme with the naturalist writers like Zola and de Maupassant who wrote grim tales about working-class people, attempting to avoid all vestiges of emotion or interpretation.

The conventions of realism are less controversial. Realist fiction attempts to present detailed, credible characters in realistic settings, engaged in action that is not dominated by coincidence, miracles or magic. The plots tend to be centred on ordinary characters going about their everyday life. The issues tend to be local rather than global and the protagonists are fallible rather than heroic. Realist texts try to convince us that their characters really did exist, and that these problems and outcomes were entirely likely in their particular settings. Writers like Fielding, Austen and Tolstoy are realists in this broad sense.

See magic realism.

realistic
A credible representation of real life.

To call a text realistic involves you in the problem of 'what is real and to whom is it real?'

See realism.

redundancy
The unnecessary repetition of an idea using a different word or words, for example: 'reversing backwards'.

See tautology.

Reformation
The period or movement in the sixteenth century in Europe in which the beliefs and practices of the Church of Rome were challenged by Martin Luther and others, leading to the development of Protestantism.

refrain
A line or lines repeated throughout a poem or song.

Renaissance
(French—'rebirth')
The period following the Middle Ages in Europe (approximately late fourteenth to the sixteenth century).

It is called a rebirth because artists and scholars revived the art and learning of Ancient Greece and Rome. There was a flowering of the arts and sciences, and a great increase in European explo ration and expansion. The period was characterised by the rise of the philosophy of humanism. The great writers of the Renaissance include: Dante and Petrarch in Italy; Montaigne and Rabelais in France; Cervantes in Spain; and Sir Thomas More, Shakespeare and Marlowe in England.

repetition
Repeating a sound, word, phrase, line or idea.

This is an important unifying element of poetry but it can also be used in prose. Techniques like rhyme, rhythm and refrains are based on repetition. The repetition of words, phrases or lines in a poem usually provides emphasis on the ideas expressed—raising their importance.

reportage
The language used by newspaper reports.

It is said that it uses no words that a twelve-year-old child wouldn't understand. It is characterised by short paragraphs, simple diction, and usually reinforces the values and beliefs of the dominant groups of the culture in which it is produced.

reported speech
Words imagined to have been said by a character or person and reported by an author. The opposite of direct speech.

representation
A construction in a text that tries to reflect some part of the real world, literally 'presenting again'.

So the characters in a novel could be seen as representations of men and women. 'Blue Heelers' is a representation of part of the Australian police force. It is a construction because these pictures are not the real Australian police but one writer's (or TV production group's) version of them.

Literary representations can either challenge or support current cultural attitudes and beliefs. They can be judged by the social consequences they may produce; by either perpetuating a prejudice against a particular group or by challenging it and causing the readers/audience to re-evaluate their own attitudes.

Student example

The representations of women in Hardy's *The Mayor of Casterbridge* are constructed around a phallocentric framework typical of Victorian England. They have little power of their own, being forced to collude with the patriarchal system in order to survive in a society hostile to women...

resistant readings/reading against the grain
A reading practice that refuses to accept the rules and assumptions of the text.

A resistant reader does not accept that the text has an obvious or natural meaning, and challenges its assumptions by focusing on its gaps, silences, and its contradictions. This is sometimes called 'reading against the grain' because it often 'gouges' sections of texts, and exposes gaps and rough edges which at first appeared to be nice and smooth.

No text is complete. No text can say everything there is to say about a subject—no matter how small. We, as readers, are invited to fill in the gaps with our accumulated knowledge from our culture, education and experience of other texts like the one we are reading. Resistant readers do not fully cooperate in these processes. Instead, they point out the values and beliefs underpinning the text, and often reject its views.

Test your understanding

Read the following text against the grain.

Extract from *Coping with Computing* (1996):

> Set up your workstation so that it allows you to work with the least strain and discomfort possible... A small room is best, away from the kids and the TV... position your computer as far to the left of the desk as possible. This will allow you some room for handwriting or perhaps a copystand. Your wife might even bring you a cup of coffee if you're lucky!... screen at eye level and a chair with supporting arms will reduce neck and shoulder strain ... allow your hand to rest comfortably on the mouse and click with your index finger...

Produce a resistant reading of this text that exposes the assumptions it makes about the following groups of people:

- kids
- computer users
- left-handers.

resolution
The events following the climax of a play or story in which the conflicts and problems raised by the plot are resolved or worked out.

See structure.

response
A reader's reaction to a text.

This includes an emotional reaction as well as an intellectual one. So a 'written response' will require an interpretation of the text as well as a discussion about its impact on the reader.

Restoration period
The period from 1660–1700.

It begins with Charles II being restored to the English throne, and is characterised by the wit and licentiousness of life in the royal court. Theatres came back to life after the austere period of the Commonwealth of Cromwell's rule.

rhetoric
The art of using language to persuade an audience.

rhetorical device
A clever arrangement of words to achieve a particular effect on the audience.

Some common rhetorical devices are the apostrophe, the rhetorical question (one that does not expect an answer) and repetition.

rhetorical question
A question that does not require an answer.

This is because the speaker or writer already assumes the answer is obvious by the context in which the question is asked. This device is sometimes used to persuade audiences by positioning them in ways that they cannot (easily) challenge. For example, see how you are positioned by this speaker who asks, 'Are we going to stand silent while our rights are ignored?'

rhyme
The occurrence of similar sounds in lines of verse.

The rhyme can occur between words at the end of lines (end-rhyme) or between words within the same line (internal rhyme).

Rhymes can be single sounds like 'flax' and 'wax' (masculine rhyme) or double rhyme like 'flower' and 'power' (feminine rhyme). Triple rhyme (or higher) tends to sound humorous, for example: 'revolution' and 'evolution'.

Rhyme performs two functions in a poem. It provides a pleasant musical effect and is itself a source of aesthetic satisfaction to the listener. It also acts to bind the lines together, to provide another element of structure in the verse. Perhaps for those bards of the oral tradition who had to remember hundreds of lines of verse, rhyme made their task a lot easier.

rhythm
The sense of movement or beat pattern in the syllables of words in a text.

In poetry the rhythm will often be a regular pattern. In prose it will usually be irregular.

See meter.

rising rhythm
A sound pattern in verse where the emphasis is thrown forward onto the last syllables of the metric feet.

In William Blake's poem 'London' the iambic and anapaestic feet have this effect:

I wander thro' each charter'd street,
Near where the charter'd Thames does flow

Romanticism
A movement in literature and arts in the period around 1750 to about 1850.

The Romantics are characterised by:

- a great interest in nature and things natural
- an association of human feelings with the changing moods of nature
- an interest in pantheism (the belief that God is in everything)
- an emphasis on the importance of the individual
- a belief in the genius and inspiration of artists
- a desire for freer and more personal expression.

Some of the best known romantics are Wordsworth, Shelley, Keats, Coleridge, Byron and Sir Walter Scott in England; Victor Hugo and Dumas in France.

saga

A lengthy tale about the exploits of heroes and kings. Most sagas are of Scandinavian origin.

sarcasm

The use of praise in a tone that clearly implies criticism, for example: 'Well done! This is the second time you've turned up to class on time this year!'

See irony.

satire

A style of writing that uses humour and exaggeration to criticise human foibles.

Satire works to portray individuals or groups or even institutions as ridiculous and thus evoke laughter and derision in the audience or reader. Unlike comedy, the final purpose of satire is to provoke thought and political change.

Jonathan Swift wrote:

> Satire is a sort of glass wherein beholders do generally discover everybody's face but their own, which is the chief reason for the kind of reception it meets in the world, and that so very few are offended with it.

His own works *Gulliver's Travels* and 'A Modest Proposal' are excellent examples of satire. In 'A Modest Proposal' Swift examines the problems brought on by the Irish potato famine. A large proportion of the population were starving and Ireland appealed to the English for help. The English saw it as a problem too difficult to deal with. Swift wrote:

> ...I shall now therefore humbly propose my own thoughts, which I hope will not be liable to the least objection.
>
> I have been assured by a very knowing American of my acquaintance in London that a young healthy child well nursed is at a year old a most delicious, nourishing and wholesome food, whether stewed, roasted, baked or boiled; and I make no doubt that it will equally serve in a fricassee or a ragout...

Student example

Muriel's Wedding satirises much of the ugly side of Australian middle-class family life. Tania's wedding scenes are humorous exaggerations of the tasteless and faithless aspects of Australian weddings. Tania thinks her puce gown is romantic; the decorations and decor are crass; the speeches are crude and insensitive and to top it all Chook (the groom) has a frantic sex scene with his new wife's best friend just after the wedding.

Test your understanding

Explain what is being satirised in the cartoon on page 88. What techniques are being used to achieve this effect?

The characters, although not often complex, are drawn in detail and the plots are normally compelling and carefully constructed. Some of the great writers in this genre are Isaac Asimov, Jules Verne, Ray Bradbury and Frank Herbert.

selection of detail

The specific events, characters and items chosen by a writer to be included in a text.

The particular details that are included (and the language in which they are described) will have a significant impact on the way the readers respond to the text and how they are positioned in relation to the subject matter.

Student example

The detail that Sonya Hartnett selects to describe the opening action of *Sleeping Dogs* establishes an emotional tone for the rest of the story. Edward is slaughtering a sheep. We are given an intimate account:

> A well-aimed blow with a mallet... snatches up his knife... pushes the bucket into position...

These details present Edward as cool and efficient. Death is something he deals with easily...

Test your understanding

Collect a number of details from a text you have read recently and explain how the inclusion of those details affected your position as a reader.

scansion

The examination and identification of the metrical patterns in verse.

scene

A sub-division of an act in a drama. Usually a scene is comprised of one main action.

science fiction

Prose narrative that includes the science and technology of some possible (or fantastic) future time.

Although science fiction is part of the fantasy genre it usually takes great pains to establish the 'reality' of the future world and its technology.

semantics

The study of the relationships between words and their meanings.

semiotics

The study of signs, particularly of language, and how communication occurs.

sense imagery

An attempt to stimulate one of the body's five senses in the description of an object, person or scene.

The five senses are:

- sight (visual imagery) 'flashing diamonds'
- hearing (auditory) 'snapping jaws'

- smell (olfactory) 'stinking carcass'
- taste (gustatory) 'sour custard'
- touch (tactile) 'velvety skin'.

To these can be added:
- sense of movement (kinetic) 'swirling water'.

Student example
Heaney evokes the smells and sounds of the muddy dam with an overpowering array of sense images:

> The slap and plop were obscene threats. Some
> sat
> Poised like mud grenades, their blunt heads
> farting.

We can hear the sounds of the frogs in these lines and begin to feel the repulsion and rising panic of the persona...

See imagery.

set
The area and background for the performance of a play or the shooting of a film.

setting
The place and context in which the events of a story occur.

There are many dimensions to the setting of a work of literature, for example: physical, social, historical, moral, psychological, etc.

The physical setting includes the geography; the climate; the landscape; and the local and domestic details of streets, houses and rooms. This is the aspect of setting that receives the most attention because it contributes a great deal to the atmosphere and tone of the text.

Student example A
The setting of *Arcadia* (Tom Stoppard) is represented as a Garden of Eden and creates a sense of luxury and decadence in the lives of the Coverleys and their guests, but also a sense of impending doom, for as we know, Adam and Eve were expelled from paradise into the desert.

Physical setting can also have a direct influence on characters and the decisions they make.

Student example B
In *The Outsider* by Camus, Meursault depicts himself as a victim of the landscape. He shot the Arab because: 'The heat was beginning to scorch my cheeks' and 'I couldn't stand it any longer...' and 'a fiery gust came from the sea...'. We almost believe that it wasn't he who pulled the trigger but a combination of heat and light and sweat.

The social setting will describe the way the characters interact—who has the power and how they use it.

Student example C
Gungee (in *A Descant for Gossips* by Thea Astley) has some clearly drawn class lines and the most dominant group are those who meet to play badminton every Sunday:

> ...that brought together in a select sporting coterie the highest income brackets in the township.

These people share similar values and become an important influence on the way residents behave.

The historical setting is also a determining factor in the way characters think, dress and behave.

Student example D
Malouf's *Remembering Babylon* begins with an amusing and alarming image that is rooted in the history of Australia's past:

> The creature...gave a kind of squawk, and leaping up onto the top rail of the fence, hung there, its arms outflung as if preparing for flight. Then the ragged mouth gapped.
>
> 'Do not shoot,' it shouted. 'I am a B-b-british object!'

We understand that this novel will give us an ironic and critical version of our past.

The moral dimension will be constructed in the way the characters treat each other and through the values they espouse.

Student example E

Moller (in *A Descant for Gossips*) finds himself in conflict with the moral code of the most powerful group in Gungee. Unfortunately for him, Findlay, his boss, is one of them:

> Findlay twitched. Moller sounded flippant, and the whole thing, the simple contravention of accepted moral code, was so important, especially in this tiny town.

This moral code is dominated by appearances and a prudish version of Christian principles...

The psychological dimension of the setting is constructed in the way the characters think and feel.

Student example F

The Well creates a claustrophobic atmosphere in which Hester is able to take control of Kathy, to regard her as her possession, something that she calls her own. The fact that the two women are isolated from outside contact on their secluded farm intensifies this atmosphere and creates a psychological reality that makes their fantasies compellingly real.

As this last example demonstrates, all these dimensions of the setting are interconnected and combined, and form the culture in which the characters operate.

Test your understanding

Using a narrative text you have read recently, write out the details of each of these dimensions of the setting of the story. Provide a specific example to illustrate each dimension.

Shakespearean sonnet

A fourteen-line poem structured in three quatrains and a final rhyming couplet.

Normally each quatrain presents a new aspect of the subject and the final couplet completes the argument or resolves any conflicts that may have been presented.

shaping

A term used in two distinct ways: the organisation or construction of a text, and the way in which readers are positioned to respond to the subject matter.

In the first usage, the emphasis is on the way the text is shaped. This involves an examination of the techniques and conventions used in the construction of the text.

In the second usage, the emphasis is on how the reader's responses are shaped by the text. This may require an examination of the values and attitudes encouraged by the text, and how particular readers respond to that encouragement.

short story

A prose fiction tale shorter than a novella.

Edgar Allen Poe (who is claimed to be the originator of the modern short story) defined it in these terms:

- it should create a single impression
- it must be capable of being read in one sitting
- every word should contribute to the overall effect
- the story should end at its climax
- the effect should be created at the opening and develop throughout the story
- only characters essential to the effect should appear.

sign
Something that stands for something else.

When a teacher claps their hands loudly it may stand for 'Silence! Give me your attention'. When the lights are flashed on and off in a supermarket it may stand for 'Please leave—we are closing soon'.

Language is also a system of signs. A word (just like the clapping of hands) is a signifier—something which points to something else. The object the word points to is called the signified. The relationship between the two is arbitrary. If it wasn't then there would only be one language in the world because the link between the signifier 'dog' and the concept to which it is pointing would be natural and essential. But of course the French use 'chien' and the Germans use 'hund', etc. If this relationship is arbitrary, how then do words have meaning?

Words have meaning not because of what they are pointing to but because of what they are not pointing to. 'Dog' means what it does because it is not pointing at the idea of cat or the idea of mouse, etc. And because it already exists in a web of other words that are pointing at similar ideas such as hound, canine and puppy.

This is important in the study of literature because the meanings of individual words and their combinations are the building blocks for our interpretations of texts.

silences
Things that are not said by the text and which the reader is not invited to examine, usually because the text does not want to expose or challenge certain cultural values or attitudes.

Student example

The film *Four Weddings and a Funeral* portrays a large number of characters who are wealthy, but do nothing to generate that wealth. This is a silence that encourages us to forget about the poor and the workers and those, in Britain, who do not have the opportunities that Charles and Scarlet and friends have. And we are invited to happily accept the system that supports such inequalities.

Test your understanding

Using a text you have read recently, locate one or more of the silences and explain why that text has remained silent on that issue.

simile
A figure of speech in which an object is compared to another in one particular aspect. This comparison is set up by using 'like' or 'as _____ as'.

Similes work best if the comparison is unexpected. Ted Hughes, in 'November' wrote:

Rain plastered the land till it was shining
like hammered lead...

And Wilfred Owen describes soldiers in the opening line of 'Dulce Et Decorum Est':

Bent double, like old beggars under sacks.

slang
A register of language associated with a particular location or occupation, more localised, more colourful, often considered more common than colloquial or formal language.

It is said that a little slang gives energy to speech but too much makes it cloying and offensive.

slapstick
Comedy that includes a lot of physical action and buffoonery such as slipping on banana skins.

slice of life
A vague term, usually meaning a kind of realism that presents life 'as it really is'.

It is a deception, of course, since writers cannot remove themselves from the writing process.

soap opera
Films, TV or radio programs that present normal everyday life as a drama.

This is a pejorative term implying that the text is melodramatic, superficial in its treatment of issues and presenting only stereotypes as characters. The label comes from the early 1930s when soap manufacturers were the main sponsors of American radio serials.

social context
The circumstances and organisation that exists in a society.

This may include the codes and conventions accepted in a group or sub-group at a particular time. In *Pride and Prejudice*, Mr Darcy breaks with the accepted practice of his social context by not joining in the dancing on his first arriving in Merrifield. This causes him to be viewed as proud and arrogant by Elizabeth and1 some of the other characters.

Readers too, will be reading in a social context which will have different conventions and may cause the reader to interpret Darcy's actions differently.

soliloquy
A speech in which a character who is usually left alone on stage delivers their thoughts and feelings on an issue.

This is a dramatic convention frequently used. Any character who delivers a soliloquy is in a privileged position, and audiences will often respond with sympathy to any character who can 'pour their heart out' and reveal their innermost desires and motives. This sympathy may not be sustained for long though as in the cases of *Macbeth* and Williamson's *The Perfectionist.*

song
Words and music combined.

Although many poems may be set to music, the poem and the song are not the same. The cultural context in which the song exists is very different from that in which the poem is read. This is especially true with modern song lyrics, and they should not be read as poems out of context. Factors to consider in the reading of a contemporary song are the image of the artists, the type of song/music, the values and beliefs associated with this style of music, the medium and its impact, the surrounding promotional material, etc.

sonnet
A form of poetry consisting of fourteen lines of iambic pentameter in a tight rhyme scheme.

The stanza pattern is usually eight/six (Petrarchan sonnet) or four/four/four/two (Shakespearean sonnet). In some modern instances twelve/two is used.

Traditionally, sonnets are dignified and controlled expressions of love or grief at the loss of a loved one. The tight structure helps to prevent the expressions becoming maudlin or indulgent.

sophistry
The use of arguments which sound convincing but are fallacious.

Spenserian sonnet
A type of fourteen-line poem with a special rhyme scheme named after the English poet Edmund Spenser.

The sonnet rhymes abab, bcbc, cdcd, ee and is sometimes call the 'link sonnet' because of the strong links between stanzas in the rhyme scheme.

Spoonerism
The speech error of switching the initial letters of words.

Named after the Reverend W. A. Spooner of New College, Oxford who is reputed to have said to one of his students:

> Sir, you have tasted your werm;
> you have hissed my mistory lectures and been caught fighting a lire in the quad;
> you will leave Oxford by the next town drain.

stage directions
Instructions in a play for actors and directors.

These instructions tell actors when to enter or exit, how to say their lines and how they might move. Recent playwrights like Harold Pinter have kept these to a bare minimum, allowing more room for interpretation by actors and directors.

stanza
A group of lines in verse.

The equivalent, perhaps, of a paragraph in prose.

stereotypes

Models or templates for a particular kind of character.

The word comes from the name of the plate (previously used in the printing industry) used to duplicate many versions of the same page.

Stereotypes often define groups in very narrow terms such as the 'dumb blonde' or the 'romantic Frenchman'. Stereotypes are used in some text types to perform a limited function in a story. For example: Perry White is the stereotype of a newspaper editor in the Superman films, performing the narrow role of the boss (usually grumpy and sceptical) for the main characters to react against.

Stereotypes can be damaging and divisive when they become the main way of thinking about a group of people. The 'dumb blonde' stereotype may be objectionable, but there are many other competing ways of thinking about females with blonde hair—such as the glamorous model or the sporting woman, etc.

These ideas are important in the study of literature and culture because readers need to be aware when they are only being offered narrow stereotypes as a basis for forming opinions.

See representation.

stock characters

Characters with a few limited characteristics, as stereotypes, often recurring in a variety of texts, for example: the clown, the nagging wife, the coward, etc.

Many of the airline disaster films of the 1970s and 1980s had a predictable passenger list, filled with stock characters such as the nervous businessman; the fading actress; a pair of nuns; a pregnant woman; and a tough, silent cop or soldier.

story

A sequence of events in chronological order.

stream of consciousness

A kind of narration that tries to capture the flow of a character's mental processes.

This includes memories, feelings, conscious and half-conscious thoughts, sense perceptions, and random associations.

Virginia Woolf used this technique quite often. Here is an example from *Mrs Dalloway*:

> She parted the curtains; she looked. Oh, but how surprising!—in the room opposite the old lady stared straight at her! She was going to bed. And the sky. It will be a solemn sky...

strophe and antistrophe

The first part of a song or address by the chorus in a Greek play.

The chorus performs the strophe while moving from one side of the stage to the other. The antistrophe is delivered while moving back to their original position.

See epode.

structuralism

A method of reading texts (or any system of signs) that focuses on the structure of the elements that make it up.

Structuralist critics look for the underlying codes and patterns in texts. Some mythic tales can be read from a structuralist perspective by observing the basic functions of their characters. The characters can participate in any of these aspects of the narrative:

- desire or objective—do they have a wish or aim to fulfil? Or, are they the character sought for?
- communication—do they provide material or information? Or, do they accept it?
- helping or hindering—do they accompany the hero or provide help? Or, are they blocking progress and must be overcome?

Student example

This is a reading of the feature film *Strictly Ballroom.*

Scott Hastings discovers his desire to dance in new ways not approved of by the establishment (Barry Fife and co.). He searches for a partner who can help him. Fran slowly becomes the dancer he is seeking and is also the one who accompanies him in his quest. Rico provides information on how to achieve his aim, by teaching him flamenco. Finally Scott and Fran perform their dance, overcoming the opposition of Fife, Tina Sparkle and the judges.

See characters.

structure

The organising framework of something.

The basic structure of an essay is the introduction, body and conclusion. The basic structure of a narrative is the exposition, complication, climax and resolution. The detailed structure is the order in which ideas or events are presented. The underlying structures of such texts are the techniques organised around oppositions such as good/bad, day/night, etc.

Student example

The basic structure of *Jack and Jill* (James Patterson) presents two sets of serial killers in the exposition, both going about their grisly activities. We also meet Alex Cross (the detective) and his family. The complication involves Cross in a difficult decision: which case should he concentrate on? When we learn that Jack and Jill are targeting the President of the USA his decision becomes even harder to make: should he protect his family and local community or the head of the nation? The climax occurs when the President is shot and the Truth School killer is captured. The resolution is short and filmic—showing Cross at home, having solved one crime but failed in the other—when the phone rings... This structure demonstrates that this novel is about a basic dilemma: which comes first—the family or the nation?

Test your understanding

Use this idea of describing the basic structure of a story in terms of the binary oppostions involved, to explain the organisation of a text you have read.

style

The way a writer uses language.

To specify a writer's style you need to examine the tone, imagery, diction, and other techniques and devices used in the text. Sometimes it may be useful to classify a writer's style by one of these methods:

- according to the period in which the text is written (such as Romantic, Augustan, metaphysical, etc.)
- according to the kind of language used (such as journalistic, scientific, poetic, didactic, etc.)
- according to the level of language used (slang, colloquial, formal).

Student example
In terms of prose style, *Day of the Dog* is like a wounded bird. It limps where it should fly, it stumbles where it should soar. The plot is both dull and unrealistic. The narrative alternates between off-hand and turgid. There are hideous lapses in continuity. If we look at *Day of the Dog* with an aesthetic reading, that there is only good writing and bad writing and no excuses, then it is obvious where *Day of the Dog* fits in. But style is not what the novel is about...

sub-genre

A sub-division of one of the literary genres.

Romance, thriller, western and fantasy are all sub-genres of the novel. This term is problematic because many readers insist that those labels are genres themselves. The reason for this confusion is because there is no standard for classifying texts into genres and sub-genres.

subject matter

The idea, issue or event at the centre of attention in a text.

sub-plot

A secondary set of actions that take place alongside the main action.

Sub-plots, like plots, must be resolved before the end of the story and this will often occur when the two areas of action meet as in the final act of Shakespeare's *King Lear*. Sub-plots often act as a reflection or counterpoint to the plot. The different plots involving Aniken Skywalker and Queen Amidala in *Star Wars, Episode 1* come together towards the end of the film.

sub-text

A meaning 'below' the text, seemingly not carried by the words themselves.

This can be constructed by readers in many ways:

- from what is not said or done
- from how things are said or done
- from a reading against the grain of the text
- from a reading of the assumptions of the text.

It is the reader's duty, says Pierre Macherey, to read the sub-text, the unspoken, the concealed and repressed—in brief the reader must try to reveal the text's unconscious content.
See assumptions.

surface features

The spelling, grammar, punctuation and paragraphing of a text.

These are the aspects of a text that should obey the prevailing codes and conventions of composition after proofreading.

surrealism

An attempt to represent the world of the unconscious mind.

The surrealists were particularly interested in dreams and semi-conscious states of mind, trying to find new knowledge and understandings of human experience. A movement in art and literature popular in the first half of the twentieth century.

suspense

(Latin—'to hang over') A technique used to keep readers wondering about the outcomes of events in a story.

The word is derived from the Latin 'to hang from or over' which brilliantly describes the feeling of tension and anticipation experienced by readers. The word 'cliff-hanger' reflects the same idea. The film of that name (starring Sylvester Stallone) demonstrated the idea quite literally.

There are two kinds of suspense—that connected with causality (whodunit?) and that connected with temporality (what will happen next?). Sir Arthur Conan Doyle uses suspense to great effect in his tales of Sherlock Holmes. In 'The Speckled Band' we are held in suspense regarding 'whodunit' and how it will end until the last possible word, when the nature of the speckled band is revealed.
See conventions of narrative.

suspension of disbelief

(willing suspension of disbelief)
Withholding judgement about the credibility of actions and characters (usually in a play).

As the audience of a play we are well aware that the actors are only pretending and that when one shoots another we should not call for the police. However, we do not view their playing or pretending in the same way that we view the games of children because we are willing to suspend our disbelief and allow ourselves to be drawn into the story and the importance of the action. We will temporarily care about what happens to the protagonist and others. Sometimes we may care so much that we are moved by their distress and cry or feel real sadness for them. We also agree to accept the conventions by which their story is presented such as the dimming of auditorium lights—meaning we should stop talking and attend to the actors.

symbol/symbolism

An object that stands for something else.

For example, the cross stands for Christianity and rosemary is for remembrance (and so is the red poppy in Australia). The problem with this idea is that the connections made between one object and the thing it stands for are not the same in every culture. And even in one culture such connections change.

Notwithstanding this, the following list of flowers are usually taken as symbols: red rose—passion; pink rose—romance; yellow rose—jealous love; white rose—pure love; daisy—dissembling or deceiving; pansy—love in vain; and columbine—faithless love.

sympathy

The conscious fellow-feeling or association with a character or person.

For example, we can quickly understand and feel for the shy student who has to get up in front of a school assembly to make a speech. In literature, readers' sympathies are often engaged by the heroes or protagonists. Their antipathy is aroused by the antagonists. For example: Batman arouses our sympathies when we learn of the story of the gunning down of his parents in cold blood. The Joker arouses our antipathy when we recognise that all his actions are motivated by an unquenchable thirst for revenge.

synaesthesia

An effect on the senses in which several senses respond to the stimulation of one.

For example, if colours are described as noisy or evoking a certain smell that is a synaesthetic effect. This is sometimes used in poetry, especially in Shelley and here, in 'Correspondances' by Baudelaire:

> There are perfumes as fresh as children's skin,
> Soft as an oboe, green as the prairies...

synecdoche

A figure of speech in which a part stands for the whole.

'All hands on deck!' means that the sailors should bring the rest of their bodies, too.

synonym

A word with the same (or similar) meaning to another.

For example, 'bloke', 'guy' and 'minor' are synonymous with 'boy' but they all have different shades of meaning.

syntagmatic/paradigmatic

Syntagmatic relationships between words are governed by the rules of combining words in a particular order—and the meanings that arise.

For example, the sentences 'Man bites dog' and 'Dog bites man' are syntagmatically different.

Paradigmatic relationships exist between words that can be substituted for each other. In the above sentences the words 'savages', 'attacks' and 'lacerates' could be substituted for 'bites', and thus have a paradigmatic relationship with each other.

syntax

The rules for the construction of a sentence.

synthesis

Bringing things together to form a whole.

This is seen as the next step after analysis. If an essay analyses a text it should also synthesise all the ideas and insights gained, to form a coherent view of the whole text. Post-modern critics would argue that this process only results in the illusion of a coherent whole, since all texts are partial and fragmentary.

See analysis, text.

Tt

tableau

Actors in a 'frozen' scene.

Tableaux are sometimes used to end a play or act. The actors take up positions and expressions appropriate to the last moment of the scene, and hold them until the curtain comes down.

tanka

A Japanese lyric composed strictly of thirty-one syllables, arranged in lines of five/seven/five/seven/seven.

The Japanese regard this as the classic form of poetry.

target audience

The readers that a text appears to be aimed at.

Some texts make this overt such as letters and diaries or texts like Jonathan Swift's 'A Modest Proposal' which is clearly directed to the English. Texts that seem to assume a 'general audience' are actually expecting a definable reader—often white, middle class and male. To define the target audience begin with the assumption that the audience is black, poor and female, and check this against the assumptions and features of the text as you read.

Test your understanding
Read the text from *Coping with Computers* on page 86 and define the target audience as specifically as you can.

tautology

The error of defining an idea in its own terms.

This is most noticeable in the repetition of the same idea in different words, for example: 'We can see that technology is dominating our lives because it is taking up too much of our time'. This can also refer to the repetition of the same idea in a phrase such as 'to ascend upwards' or 'the main protagonist'.

techniques

In the study of texts this refers to the devices and methods used in the construction of texts.

In narrative texts, the main techniques are plot, characterisation, setting, point of view and diction. In poetry, the main techniques used are sound devices, imagery, form, etc. In drama texts, the main techniques used are plot, characterisation, dialogue, set, action and costumes. In film and TV texts, the main techniques used are plot, characterisation, dialogue, set, camera work, lighting and sound. Some texts will, of course, make use of other techniques and perhaps avoid using some of these altogether, for example Ted Hughes's story 'Snow' may be said to lack setting (although others may argue that this is the most powerful element in the story!). 'The Crime in the Attic' by Enrique Anderson Imbert is a short story without plot or characters. Many contemporary writers have experimented with the form of a genre by varying the way these techniques are used—with varying success.

In the critical study of texts, it is important to be able to recognise techniques in texts, but it is more important to be able to explain how they position and affect readers.

See conventions.

text

(Latin—'a woven fabric')

There are a number of different meanings:

- a construction in language from which readers can construct meaning through a system of shared conventions
- the actual words on the page
- a book recommended for study
- anything from which meaning can be made.

By this last definition a photograph, park, beach or even clothes can be texts. This is justified on the basis that readers of these objects can construct meanings by reading the codes and conventions by which they were constructed. Roland Barthes has made the distinction between a text that is lisible (readable) because it conforms to the prevailing codes and conventions, and a text that is illisible (unreadable) because it defies or ignores those conventions such as James Joyce's *Finnegan's Wake*, or the poetry of some of the experimental poets such as Michael McClure's 'Grahhh! Michael in the lion's den' which is dominated by a collection of roars and growls. These texts shock and frustrate our expectations, and disrupt our attempts to create meaning.

Most contemporary critics agree that texts have the following features:

- they are human constructs, not natural occurrences
- they are made up of individual items whose meaning depends on their relation with other items
- they make sense within a system of codes and conventions shared by people who can read them.

text's context

The surrounding circumstances of a text or part of a text.

A text exists in a culture and within a web of other texts—in a relationship with some texts that are similar and many that are different. It is because of these relationships that readers can make sense of a particular text or fragment.

textual criticism

The work of a critic who reads and evaluates original manuscripts to decide what final version was intended.

theatre

The auditorium or arena in which a play is performed in front of an audience.

These can range from the Ancient Greek style amphitheatre, open-air stages, proscenium arch, theatre-in-the-round through to public squares or streets. The word theatre also describes the kind of play that is performed, as in Theatre of the Absurd and Theatre of Cruelty.

Theatre of the Absurd

A term used to describe some of the drama of the twentieth century that presents life as meaningless and absurd.

Often these plays are seen as controversial, not only because of their content, but also because they abandon the normal conventions of drama such as not having a well-developed plot or presenting characters whose actions and motivations are not consistent.

The two tramps in Samuel Beckett's play *Waiting for Godot* exemplify the sense of isolation and abandonment felt by many of the characters in this kind of theatre:

Vladimir: ...Gogo.
Estragon: What?
Vladimir: Suppose we repented.
Estragon: Repented what?
Vladimir: Oh...(He reflects.) We wouldn't have to go into the details.
Estragon: Our being born?
(Vladimir breaks into a hearty laugh which he immediately stifles...)

See absurdism.

Theatre of Cruelty

A kind of drama that attempts to deeply disturb the audience both intellectually and emotionally so that each person is forced to see themselves as they really are.

The French dramatist Antonin Artaud published his principles in 1938, in which he described the means and reasons for such an approach.

theme

The central idea of a text.

This is not the subject but a claim or argument that the text puts forward. It may be implicit or clearly stated. Some critics insist that a theme should be 'a statement about the human condition'. Others argue that this is a restrictive and one-dimensional approach since it seems to suggest that there are universal, shared aspects of the human condition, that anyone, in any culture, at any time, would recognise; and that there is one theme embedded in the text that every reader would be able to discover.

Post-modernists argue that if there are themes or central ideas in texts then different groups of readers will find different ones because of their differing beliefs and reading practices.

See issue/theme.

thesis

A proposition or idea set down to be demonstrated by the argument which follows.

third person point of view

The voice of a persona telling a story in which they are not a character. This voice is not the author.

See narrator.

tone

The way language is used to reflect attitudes to the subject matter and the readers.

If the text is spoken (or imagined as spoken) then the volume, pitch, timbre, emphasis and intonation will carry the tone. Readers or listeners will judge tone from past experience and from the contextual clues, such as in Faye Weldon's *Female Friends* (1975):

> She loves him. Oh, indeed she does. Her heart quickens at the sight of him, her bowels dissolve with longing.

This is either serious and melodramatic in tone (from a Mills and Boon romance novel?), or it is parodic and is not taking the characters seriously. Readers will decide which is the case from the surrounding text.

The following are a list of common words used to describe tone: serious; sombre; ironic; satiric; parodic; bitter; sarcastic; melodramatic; cynical; critical; knowledgeable; laconic; excited; mournful; forceful; wise; guarded; ominous; proud; sincere; light-hearted; didactic; and flippant.

topic sentence

The sentence that carries the main idea of a paragraph.

Topic sentences can appear anywhere in a paragraph but the rest of the paragraph will expand on the idea contained in the topic sentence.

tragedy

Stories (usually in the form of drama) in which serious and important actions turn out disastrously for the main character.

In Greek tragedy this is because the tragic hero is led by their hamartia (tragic flaw) to say or do something that will lead to their downfall. Aristotle's definition of tragedy (*see* Greek tragedy) is still the first reference point today. His idea of defining the form by referring to its effects on the audience is controversial—especially his idea of catharsis—the 'purgation' or 'purification' of the emotions of those in the audience. This is the effect that leaves an audience feeling not depressed at the hero's suffering and defeat, but relieved and even inspired at the end of the play. But some critics have reduced this to 'feeling better after a good cry'.

Tragedies of the late sixteenth century and the early seventeenth century (Shakespeare, Marlowe, Webster) varied from the classical Greek and Roman model and worked out new conventions for themselves.

Some critics see Macbeth as not a good and noble man who commits a tragic error, but an ambitious man who premeditatedly murders his king and friends so that he deserves his destruction at the hand of the more admirable Macduff. Many of Shakespeare's plays also deviate from the classical formula by including comical scenes.

By the end of the nineteenth century tragedy had undergone another change. Ibsen and Strindberg (two Scandinavian dramatists) wrote plays that revealed a society that was corrupt and diseased—and their 'tragic heroes' were now neither people of high standing (generals or princes) nor male. Some of their plays caused great public outcry—possibly because their vision was too close to the truth.

In the twentieth century the tragic drama has been significantly influenced by the Theatre of the Absurd. Now tragedy portrays the grief and suffering of the ordinary person—the most notable protagonists have been peasants, tramps, a salesman and a caretaker. To represent these subjects the dramatists have used understatement and colloquial language. They have often represented the inarticulateness of their characters and focused on their lack of ability to actually listen or talk to each other. There is a huge chasm between the moving final speech of Othello and the barely coherent ramblings of Davies in the final scene of Pinter's *The Caretaker*.

The novel can also be viewed as a tragedy. Thomas Hardy's novel *The Mayor of Casterbridge* presents a man of intellect and strength who, in a moment of weakness, sells his wife for an alcoholic drink. *The Wife of Martin Guerre* by Janet Lewis presents a woman who destroys her family in her obsessive search for the truth.

The question remains for all these modern texts—are they tragedies by Aristotle's definition? And if not, are they tragedies in any sense?

tragi-comedy
A type of drama that mixes the subjects and forms of both tragedy and comedy.

Both characters of high and low degree can be portrayed, and the plot may promise terrible outcomes but end happily. Shakespeare's *Merchant of Venice* is a good example where nobility (the Duke of Venice) mix with commoners (Shylock the money-lender), and the possible tragic outcome (Antonio's death) is avoided, and lovers and their possessions are re-united.

tragic flaw
The error of judgement or momentary lapse of reason in a tragic hero that leads to their downfall and destruction.

Aristotle called this 'hamartia'. This should not be a consistent character fault since the tragic hero must maintain a status of being better than we are, especially in the moral sense, so that their fall might effectively evoke our pity and our terror.

See Greek tragedy.

tragic hero
The principal character in a tragedy who begins in a position of social importance (a king or prince or general) and who is held in high esteem, but through an error of judgement brings about their own downfall and destruction.

Whether modern tragedies like *Death of a Salesman* or *The Caretaker* present tragic heroes or not is still a matter of debate—salesmen and caretakers do not occupy positions of social importance and so their downfall is of limited significance. Also, these characters tend to be ordinary, flawed individuals whose suffering might not be described as undeserved.

tragic irony
A situation in a story where a character does not know a vital piece of information that the audience does know.

When, because of this, the character does or says something which the audience knows will lead to disaster that is a tragic irony.

See dramatic irony.

transactional text
A text that conveys information.

A transactional text is therefore usually expository rather than narrative.

translation
Rewriting a text into another language.

This is always a problem for readers who cannot read the original text as Susan Midalia points out in 'Textualising Gender' (1999):

> In *The Lost Honour of Katerina Blum* (H. Boll) 'bang' is used by the sexually predatory male journalist to describe what he wants to do to the heroine, and the word is then appropriated by Katerina, who turns it into the 'bang' of the pistol as she shoots him dead... I'm assuming, by the way, that the pun works in the original German. If it doesn't, then my argument is, so to speak, shot...

travesty
***See* burlesque.**

trilogy
A group of three texts claiming unity.

The original trilogies were Ancient Greek tragedies presented at the religious festivals in the fifth century BC. *The Oresteia* by Aeschylus is the earliest surviving example. Recently, the term is most commonly used to describe a set of three novels.

Tudor period
The period 1485–1603 during which the monarchs of England all came from the Tudor family.

This was a time of great activity in literature and art, especially in the latter half of this period.

TV drama
Any of a wide range of television fictions.

Boundaries between TV serials and TV drama series have become blurred and even the TV 'soapie' is no longer easily identified since writers and producers have become more and more experimental in their manipulation of these forms. Recent productions like 'Wildside', 'Frontline' and 'Neon Genesis Evangelion' challenge the boundaries of these categories.

Uu

understatement

Representing something as much less in magnitude or importance than it really is.

Mark Twain's comment: 'The reports of my death are greatly exaggerated' is an example. Also the laconic response of Joe Brown in the film *Some Like It Hot* when he is told that his bride-to-be is a man: 'Well, nobody's perfect'.

unities

The three unities are devices to create (on stage) an effect of a convincing reality or the illusion of reality in the audience.

Unity of action was one of Aristotle's recommendations—that a play should concentrate on one action. The test of this is that if any part of the play was to be deleted then the whole play would be altered and the worse for it.

Unity of time was added in the sixteenth century to indicate that the whole action of the play should take place within one day—or part of a day.

Unity of place means that the action should occur in one place only. These devices were not as popular in Britain as they were in Europe since Shakespeare's plays did not adhere to these conventions. In modern drama these conventions have been largely ignored.

unity

The notion that a text has a coherence and completeness so that each part is necessary and inter-dependent, forming a part of the perfect whole.

Postmodern critics consider this idea quaint, since they argue that every text is:

- partial and fragmentary—it must leave gaps and silences because it cannot say everything
- ambiguous—since the meanings are partially dependent on the readers
- contradictory—since they assert more than one idea and depend on readers for interpretations.

Texts appear to be unified because readers have been taught to look for unity in texts.

universality

The quality of a text that is thought to transcend the specific details of time, place and individuals, to be applicable to all people at any time in any place.

This means that the text will be concerned with aspects of human experience that never change such as the seven deadly sins (pride, avarice, envy, lust, gluttony, sloth and wrath).

Postmodern critics question this notion that any text can be universal—since readers construct meanings within the rules and boundaries of their own culture, and those rules and practices can vary widely.

utopia/dystopia

Utopia is a perfect (imaginary) society.

It is the title of a book written by Sir Thomas More in 1516. There have been many books written presenting these ideal visions, including H. G. Wells's *Men Like Gods* and *A Modern Utopia* (1905), and Samuel Butler's *Erehwon*.

A dystopia is the opposite of a utopia—a society that is functioning against the interests of its citizens. There are many versions of these kinds of society in literature including Margaret Atwood's *The Handmaid's Tale*, George Orwell's *Nineteen Eighty-Four* and Aldous Huxley's *Brave New World*.

Vv

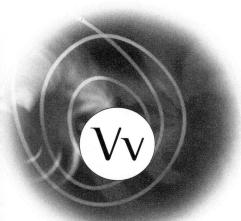

values
A subjective assessment of an issue turned into a principle, based on an individual's or group's beliefs.

Another way of thinking of values is the ideals or standards upon which actions are based. For example: in relation to abortion one person may hold the value that 'life is more important than anything else'. Another person may hold the value: 'A woman must retain the right to decide what happens to her own body'. These people may find themselves in a clash of values.

A series of value judgements such as these constitute an individual's value system. In *Lord of the Flies*, the boys value their ritual hunt; the excitement and togetherness that it produces over the life of Ralph or any individual. When the naval officer at the end of the novel reasserts the values and order of the outside world we are challenged by the text to ask ourselves exactly how far those values differ from those of the boys.

Test your understanding
Read the student example responding to E. P. France on page 13 (*see* bias). Describe the values of each of these readers.

See attitude.

verbal irony
An effect that occurs when a statement's implied meaning is different to its explicit meaning.

See irony.

verisimilitude
Likeness to the truth.

Even fantasy and science fiction can attain verisimilitude by convincing readers that their worlds are rooted in the real. Whether a text does this or not depends not so much on the subject matter but on the skill with which the text uses the conventions and techniques of the genre.

See realism.

vernacular
The language of your native country.

This is often used in contrast with the Latin used by the Christian Church for many centuries.

verse
There are two important meanings: a line or a stanza in poetry (used as a substitute for 'stanza') and poetry.

To call poetry 'verse' is sometimes seen as pejorative—an insult, because poetry is thought to be better crafted than verse.

vers libre
Free verse.

A term derived from the French to describe the experimental verse of around 1880 onwards.

Victorian period
The time covering the reign of Queen Victoria in England, 1837–1901.

This was a time in which the novel changed and developed greatly.

vignette

A small scene that draws attention to itself by its sense of completeness (even though it forms part of a larger text).

See unity.

villanelle

A strict form of poetry that uses five three-line stanzas and a final quatrain.

The first and third lines of the first stanza must be repeated alternately in the following stanzas and form a final couplet. Dylan Thomas's 'Do Not Go Gentle into That Good Night' is an example of the villanelle. The final couplet is:

> Do not go gentle into that good night.
> Rage, rage against the dying of the light.

voice

The sense of the personality and intelligence behind the words of a text.

This term is sometimes used to describe the persona or narrator of a text but is more correctly aimed at describing that presence beyond the fictitious voices in a work. Some critics call this the implied author.

Student example A

There is an arrogance and pride behind the words of Cecil Rhodes:

> Remember that you are an Englishman, and have consequently won first prize in the lottery of life.

This voice reminds us of the superiority implied by Adolph Hitler when he said:

> The great masses of the people... will more easily fall victims to a great lie than to a small one.

Student example B

Despite the awkward prose and the high-ground morality of the narrative voice, a reading of *Day of the Dog* from the point of view of social consciousness sees it as a powerful early attempt by Archie Weller to find his own voice and to reach those who share his experience. His didactic narrative voice disables much of what he says, perhaps because, as a storyteller, he too has taken the city, rather than his own people as his elder.

Test your understanding

Read one of your own essays or exam papers. What features does this voice have? What can you do to make the voice of this persona more engaging? If you find this exercise too difficult, then swap essays with a friend and help each other to improve the voice in your writing.

See persona.

volta

The transition between the octave and the sestet in a sonnet. The volta is a pause before the new thought of the second stanza.

See caesura.

weltschmerz

A weariness with life.

This is sometimes displayed in the literature of the fifteenth century and in some of the works of the existentialists like Albert Camus. *A Happy Death* is an example:

> To be so far away from everything, even from his fever, to suffer here what was so absurd and miserable ... Around him the flaccid hours lapped like a stagnant pond—time had gone slack ...

wit

The ability to express a fine idea with precision and perhaps humour.

The meaning of this word has changed significantly over time. In the Middle Ages it meant 'senses' as in our five senses. These were referred to as our 'five wits'.

During the Renaissance it meant 'intelligence' or even 'genius' as in the phrase 'to be quick-witted'.

In the seventeenth century it meant 'fancy' or 'imagination'. So when the metaphysical poets are praised for their 'wit' it is for their ability to create fanciful conceits like John Donne's image of the twin compasses to describe his relationship with his lover/wife in the poem 'A Valediction: Forbidding Mourning'.

In recent times the word is associated with humour, although such humour must be subtle and clever as well, as in 'a witty remark'.

See epigram.

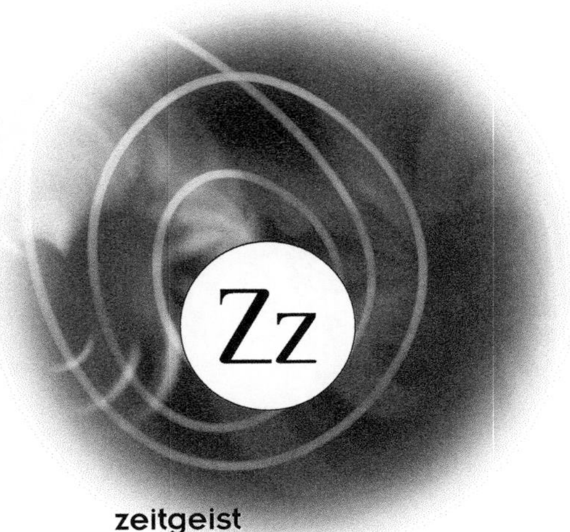

zeitgeist
The spirit of the times.

The zeitgeist of the 1960s might have been encapsulated by 'Peace and Love'. The zeitgeist of today might be captured by the term 'economic rationalism'.

Index

Index of authors cited

Index

Index of films cited